SEA SHELLS OF THE WORLD

Christmas 1970

To Reha,
with all good wishes.
from Joan.

SEA SHELLS
OF THE WORLD

BY

A. GORDON MELVIN, PH.D

Photographs by Lorna Strong Melvin

CHARLES E. TUTTLE CO.: PUBLISHERS
Rutland, Vermont & Tokyo, Japan

Representatives:

For Continental Europe:
BOXERBOOKS, INC., Zurich

For the British Isles:
PRENTICE-HALL INTERNATIONAL, INC., London

For Australasia:
PAUL FLESCH & CO., PTY. LTD., Melbourne

For Canada:
M. G. HURTIG LTD., Edmonton

Published by the Charles E. Tuttle Company, Inc.
of Rutland, Vermont & Tokyo, Japan
with editorial offices at
Suido 1-chome, 2-6, Bunkyo-ku, Tokyo

Library of Congress Catalog Card No. 66-18967

Standard Book No. 8048 0512-1

First Printing, 1966

Sixth Printing, 1970

Book design by Simon Virgo
PRINTED IN JAPAN

Contents

INTRODUCTION

USES OF THIS BOOK

THIS IS A practical book for shell collectors rather than a contribution to pure science. It is primarily for use by that army of enthusiasts who have a personal interest in shells, for those who tend to be fascinated by shells as gifts of nature. Such people are usually less concerned with the whole animal of which the shell is a part than with the shell itself. In shells one may discover intellectual, aesthetic, personal, or social values. Shell collecting is an avocation which offers wide and varied experience. It provides endless hours with the shells themselves and with books and articles about them, leads to outdoor activity, and gives a reason to travel to both local and distant parts. In addition, collecting keeps one in touch by correspondence with people of other countries and brings about companionship with those of related interest at home. In fact, shells usually lead to interesting contacts because when one meets a shell collector, one generally meets a person worth knowing.

This book is offered not to professional malacologists but to the vast number of shell collectors and shell fanciers, a group which seems to be increasing rapidly. Consequently, in every aspect of this presentation, practical considerations have taken precedence over scientific ones. It is hoped, nevertheless, that within this framework, scientific matters have been considered carefully and the contributions of science used as well and as fully as possible. Thus while this book may not be called a scientific book, it is hoped that it is not an unscientific one.

WHAT SHELLS HAVE BEEN PHOTOGRAPHED HERE?

IN PREPARING this book the writer has kept one thing in mind above all else. This has been to offer what would be most needed by a collector of world shells in his first, and perhaps only, book on shells. More than anything else, a collector needs a book picturing and describing a selection of available shells chosen from the species most wanted by active

collectors. An attempt has been made here to provide this within the scope of these pages. It has been necessary to discriminate in the selection of shells covered in an effort to curtail the size of the book so that the price could remain within the reach of every serious collector. The high cost of publishing, especially of material in color, has made the price of some of the best books on shells beyond the reach of many of us. Most of these books, although complete in their own area, cover but a segment of the world's shells, so that the collector must obtain about ten such volumes in order to have comprehensive material. In this book an attempt has been made to crosscut these areas selectively so as to give the collector with, at first, only one book the guidance he needs and the information he will continue to want to refer to. It is hoped that this volume will prove indispensable to its owner as long as he continues to be interested in shells.

About half the shells have been photographed in color; the rest in black and white. This has affected the way in which the book is organized, since an attempt has been made to show in color those shells in which color is a particularly important feature. But color is not a main feature in most shells, and, within the framework of practicality, those shells in which form rather than color is most important have been photographed in black and white. Various well-known shells have been omitted for one reason or another, usually because of the unavailability of a good specimen at the time of photographing. The placing of species in the plates has occasionally been determined by when the shell was at hand to be photographed. Like many other authors, this one has succumbed to the temptation to show, at times, unusually fine specimens. Such specimens are often scarce and hard to obtain for someone who wants one "just like the picture." Still, these make for more interesting and helpful photographs.

NAMES OF SHELLS

AUTHORITIES on shell classification and naming are by no means in agreement on the names of all shells. There is, as yet, no accepted world adjudication on what is a final correct naming of groups or species, and names continue to change. Recently, much new and more exact information has been coming in as a result of malacologists' research, changing names more rapidly than ever. Seeing an old favorite with a new

name often gives collectors a feeling of sadness and frustration. This book, therefore, has not made it a chief aim to give the most correct, most recent, or most temporarily fashionable name at the time of publication. Much care has been given to correct naming, but whenever there has been a conflict between seeming authority and practicality for the collector using this book, the practical method has been followed. This has affected both the style used in presenting the names and the names themselves. As to style, wherever it has seemed advisable, this book has adopted its own style. The rule followed for the names has been to present the name in the form most likely to be helpful to the reader. For instance, a very popular shell owned by most collectors is listed here as *Cassis (Phalium) strigata* Gmel. This shell is known to many as *Phalium strigata* Gmelin, but the generic name *Phalium* gives the amateur no key to the fact that this shell belongs to the same family as *Cassis cornuta* L. Both shells are *Cassidae*, but the generic name *Phalium* for the former indicates only the special sub-division of the very large family *Cassidae* to which this shell belongs. On the other hand, another member of the family *Cassidae* is listed by the name by which it has become familiar to collectors, *Cassis testiculus* L., the Baby Bonnet. In other words, this book is deliberately incon-sistent in terms of naming because the author has in each case decided for himself what name will best serve the collector until such time as the latter wishes to make a study of naming by consulting other books and reference material. The name given to a shell by the earliest author who publishes a description of it is regarded by authorities as the correct name. Consequently, a familiar name is sometimes replaced when a scientific researcher discovers from older documents that the shell has been earlier described under another name. The older name then takes precedence. But there is a convenient rule followed by some malacol-ogists which allows a name which has been undisturbed for fifty years, and so become widely used, to remain even if it is discovered that the shell had been described under a different name by some earlier author.

It should be of some comfort to a collector that no matter what label is attached, the shell remains the same shell. At the same time, one is free to change the label to one's heart's content, as often as one likes, and in any way one likes. There is no law that a collector must follow the dictates of science in naming his shells. He does so only for his own convenience and the convenience of others. Even if one had in one's

collection a venerable item on which the name *Pterocera aurantia* Lam. had been crossed out and the name *Lambis aurantia* put in, and on which that name had again been crossed out and replaced by the current name *Lambis crocata* Link, yet under all these various labels it remains just that same specimen. Let us never worry about which label is most correct! Any name by which the shell has been called, if the author-name is given, is a good name. Being consistently practical in the interest of collectors is the only consistency to be expected in this book. The writer bows to sound criticism, but will not be alarmed by it.

Common names have no standing in any circles of importance since Latin names are the only ones that serve all collectors in every country in our grand world of man-made border lines. Common names differ from time to time and place to place. In fact, you may give a shell any common name you like and put on it your own label. Quite gratuitously I have called that favorite of many collectors, the Japanese *Thatcheria mirabilis* Angas, the Wonder Shell, my own translation of the Latin. But some shells have common names which have been widely used for a long time. When it has seemed useful, these names have been given here for what value they may have. The name Angel Wing, for instance, for *Barnea costata* L. is so apt that we use it freely.

WHY PRICES AND WHAT DO THEY MEAN?

PRICES ARE given in this book as a matter of convenient information only. In no sense is this book an offer by either the author or the publisher of shells for sale. Shells can be obtained by collecting them, exchanging them, or by buying them from dealers. The author will arrange to have a dealer's list sent to anyone who sends him a stamped addressed envelope. Prices may appear high, but in actual fact the writer knows of no dealer who supports himself solely by the sale of specimen shells. One writer has recently stated that the way to select a shell is to get lists from a number of dealers and then buy from the one who offers the particular shell at the lowest price. This is very bad advice since shells of a given species differ vastly in quality. Actually, one should select a dealer who is scrupulously honest and who prices shells in terms of their quality. It is best to buy from a dealer who sends out shells in the condition and of the quality one prefers. If the shells can actually be seen when they are purchased, this is best of all.

The prices given here are inexact, based on the prices at which shells usually have been sold by dealers in the five years preceding the date of publication of this book. Like diamonds, shells are found free in nature for the taking and acquire value, and so price, by what has happened to them subsequent to their being found. Value depends on many factors: the economics of the country in which the shell is found, the temporary or permanent scarcity of specimens, and the difficulty of access depending on shallow or deep water or consequent problems of diving or dredging. Dredging is a very expensive process, and dredged shells may be costly. At any given time, there is an approximate value currently accepted by dealers and arrived at in relation to the particular shell's scarcity, demand, and quality. In ten good specimens, one will be more perfect than the others and command a higher price, although shell buyers often expect to get the best specimen at the average price.

Providing suggested prices has been one of the most difficult aspects of writing this book. Yet the task was undertaken because by giving the approximate current value of shells, the usefulness of this book to collectors has been more than doubled. There is no possible way in which, by merely looking at a shell or at its picture, one can tell the market value of the shell. For example, I recently received from the Philippines a superb *Cypraea carneola* L. which is about the same size as a normal *Cypraea aurantium* Gmel.; but the cost of the former, known as the Carnelian Cowry, is about $2.00, while the cost of the latter, known as the Golden Cowry, fresh-caught from Fiji is about $150.00. Neither can the collector tell the correct market value of a shell by consulting a dealer's list because he then has no way of knowing what the shell is likely to be priced elsewhere. Of the hundreds of scientific text books available, none gives prices. This leaves the collector unguided in a matter of serious practical concern which bears not merely on purchases but also on exchanges. It is because of these circumstances that the present book gives the approximate prices prevailing at the time of publication of Grade A specimens.

It is important to point out, however, that the prices of shells, as of all commodities, vary. A magazine reports that it found exactly the same electrical appliance of the same brand priced in different stores variously at $28.50, $34.50, and $58.00. Similarly, an acquaintance found a Golden Cowry in a thrift shop on Cape Cod and bought it for $2.00, a tiny fraction of the usual price. Prices listed here, therefore, should

not be regarded as final or absolutely fixed as this is not a sales catalogue, but these figures are intended as a guide to the collector.

The prices listed are dealers' prices, not dockside prices. Tourists visiting the ports in West Mexico, Australia, the Philippines, and Fiji often buy shells from the local fishermen and divers. I frequently get letters from these countries reporting that these tourists, without thinking what they are doing, pay fishermen disproportionately high prices, making all tourists appear gullible. Beach buyers do not realize that much of the retail cost of a shell comes from the fact that it has passed from fisherman to supplier, supplier to dealer, and dealer to collector, each one having to be paid for his costs, space, and time. As a general rule, tourists might expect to take advantage of being on the spot to the extent of expecting a 50% reduction on prices listed here. Even at that, they could still regard themselves as being generous.

PHOTOGRAPHS

THE PHOTOGRAPHS in this book were all taken by my wife with a Rolleiflex, usually with cross-lighting of two photoflood lamps and with the specimens placed on black velvet. Focusing problems made it necessary that a single plate show mostly shells of a similar size, preventing the customary arrangement of shells in their scientific sequence. Drawings, which are used in many shell books, would have eliminated this difficulty, but it was felt to be of primary importance that the book be composed entirely of actual photographs of the shells. Within the limits possible, the scientific order and sequence have been followed.

One must actually have a shell to photograph it. Most of the shells shown here are in our family collection, a collection built on that of my wife's father, Alden Strong, who originally interested us both in shells. Upward of sixty specimens were loaned to me by my friends, Mr. and Mrs. F. Knight Hadley. Access to their library and to their superb collection has been an inestimable aid. For the most part, however, it has been necessary to go it alone, and the mistakes and shortcomings incidental to such a complex piece of work are mine and mine only. For these I offer my humble apologies.

A. Gordon Melvin

863 Watertown St.,
West Newton
Mass. 02165

SEA SHELLS OF THE WORLD

Plate 1

1. *Patella tabularis* Krauss. S.Afr. Reddish and ribbed. Largest of the S. African limpets. To 5¾".   4" 2.75

2. *Acmaea testudinalis* Müller. Labr. to Conn. Brown edges. "Owl" patch within.   1" .25

3. *Patella granatina* L. S.Afr. Garnet Limpet. Dark patch inside.   2½" 1.00

4. *Patella radians* Gmel. N.Zeal. Glistening interior. See also No. 20.   1¼" .50

5. *Fissurella picta* Gmel. Peru. Rayed.   2¾" 1.50

6. *Patella eucosmia* Pilsbry. Japan. Thin white horseshoe on rich brown.   1⅛" .25

7. *Patella longicosta* Lam. S.Afr. Spider-shaped with brown "footprint."   2½" 1.25

8. *Patella astera* Lam. Bombay. Yellowish. Brown marginal wedges.   1¼" .50

9. *Patella nigrolineata* Reeve. Japan. Dark lines radiate from red-brown patch.   1¾" .50

10. *Patella miniata* Born. S.Afr. Badge-shaped. White ribs on reddish or brownish. Flat, close ribbing. See also No. 24.   2½" 1.00

11. *Patella variegata* Blainville. N.S.W., Aust. Pattern and color variations. See also No. 12.   1½" .50

12. *Patella variegata* Blainville. N.S.W., Aust. See also No. 11.   1½" .50

13. *Patella testudinaria* L. P.I. Resembles tortoise shell.   2¼" .75

14. *Patella oculus* Born. S.Afr. Eye-like, colorful interior rings.   2" 1.00

15. *Patella limbata* Phil. Tasmania. Fine interior color of yellows to coral.   2" 1.00

16. *Patella argentata* Sow. Hawaii. High. Marginal interior ring silvered.   3" 2.00

17. *Megathura crenulata* Sow. Calif. to Mex. Greenish grey. White inside. Usually lacks red growth shown.   3½" .75

18. *Lottia gigantea* Gray. Calif. to Mex. Owl Limpet. Can be polished.   2½" .65

19. *Umbraculum indica* von Martens. E.Afr. & Mauritius. Flattish and shiny. Interior brown patch on yellow.   2¼" 1.00

20. *Patella radians* Gmel. N.Zeal. High. Dark ribs. Variable. See also No. 4.   1¼" .50

21. *Patella granularis* Reeve. S.Afr. Ribs bear scales.   2" .75

22. *Acmaea diaphana* Nuttal. Peru. Brown, in and out. White flecks. Semi-translucent.   1" .75

23. *Patella cochlear* Born. S.Afr. Ear or Spoon Limpet. Smaller ones grow on larger. Bluish. Dark edge and horseshoe around scar.   1¾" .75

24. *Patella miniata* Born. S.Afr. Young. See also No. 10. Red or brown.   1¼" .40

25. *Patella aenea* Gmel. Patagonia, S. Amer. Brown. White rings. Metallic inside and out.   2½" 1.50

26. *Patella radians flava* Hutton. Hawkes Bay, N. Zeal. Salmon in and out. Glistens.   1¼" .50

27. *Siphonaria pectinata* L. Miami, Fla. Syn: *S. naufragum* Stearns. White, opalescent ring, surrounded by tortoise-shell markings.   2" .75

PLATE 1

Plate 2

1. *Nerita polita* L. Pac. Grey or with red bands. ¾″—1½″ ¾″ .25

2. *Aplustrum amplustre* L. P.I. Ship's Flag. Dark bands on color. ½″ .50

3. *Phos senticosus* L. P.I. Finely ridged. 1″ .35

4. *Spirula spirula* Lam. World Seas. Ram's Horn. ¾″ .40

5. *Phos candei* d'Orb. N.C. to W.I. Net of ridges. 1″ 1.00

6. *Clanculus puniceus* Phil. E.Afr. Strawberry Shell. ¾″ .75

7. *Nerita peleronta* L. Fla. to W.I. Famed Bleeding Tooth. ½″—1½″. .10—.35

8. *Cancellaria cancellata* Lam. N.W.Afr. 1″ 2.00

9. *Phasianella ventricosa* Swain. S.Aust. One of the Pheasant Shells. 1½″ 1.50

10. *Janthina janthina* L. Warm World Seas. Syn: *J. fragilis* Lam. Floats on its raft of eggs. One of the much-liked Violet Snails. Often beached by storms. 1″ .50

11. *Monodonta obtusa* Dillwyn. Queensland, Aust. See also No. 13. 1¼″ 2 for .25

12. *Apollon gyrinus* L. Aust. Brown, noduled bands. 1″ 1.00

13. *Monodonta obtusa* Dillwyn. Queensland, Aust. See also No. 11. 1¼″ 2 for .25

14. *Natica canrena* L. Fla. Spotted Bull's Eye. 1½″ .50, 2″ 1.00

15. *Natica aurantia* Lam. P.I. Yellow to golden. 1½″ 1.00

16. *Natica onca* Röd. E.Afr. An umbilical sinus. 1″ .35

17. *Monodonta labio* L. Indo-Pac. One tooth. Pearly inside. ¾″ .25

18. *Cerithidea montagnei* d'Orb. Panamic Prov. Curved, axial ribs. 1½″ .60

19. *Lischkeia argenteonitens* Lisch. Japan. Pearled specimen. Iridescent. 2″ .75

20. *Columbarium pagoda* Less. Japan. Famed Pagoda Shell. 2″ .50, 3″ 1.00

21. *Turbo imperialis* Gmel. Ind. Oc. Polished to show pearl, green, and white. 2″ 1.00

22. *Cassis vibex* L. Pac. Shiny. Stripes on lip. 2″—3″ .50—.75

23. *Nassa sertum* Brug. Pac. Syn: *Iopas sertum* Brug. Valued because it was only species in its genus. 1½″ .60

24. *Architectonica perspectiva* L. P.I. Spiral color bands. 1½″ 1.00

25. *Architectonica nobilis* Röd. Fla. Syn: *A. granulata* Lam. Granulated spirals. 1¼″ 1.00

26. *Trochus maculatus* Lam. P.I. Green mottling. 1¼″ .50

27. *Drupa ricinus albolabris* Lam. E.Afr. Black squares on orange. Spines on lip. ¾″ .50

28. *Murex gemma* Sow. Calif. Gem Murex. Neat black on white. 1¼″ .75

29. *Apollon perca* Perry. Japan. Maple Leaf or Winged Frog. Same as *Ranella pulchra* Gray. 1¾″ .30, higher for perfect tips

30. *Echinellopsis grandinatus* P.I. Pink, brown, and white. 1″ .25

31. *Fusinus niponicus* Smith. Japan. Line-like nodules on axial lines. 1½″ .40

32. *Calliostoma (Maurea) punctulata* Mart. N.Zeal. Brown over iridescent pearl. 1″ .75

33. *Acanthina brevidentata* Wood. Panamic Prov. Syns: *Purpura cornigera* Blainville, *P. ocellata* Kiener, and *Monoceros maculatum* Gray. Bands of white squares on black. 1″ .50

34. *Ricinula ricinus* L. E.Afr. Bands of brown squares. Ribbed teeth 1″ .40

35. *Drupa morum* Röd. P.I. Syn: *D. horrida* Lam. Bands of brown nodules. Purple along opening. 1½″ .75

36. *Drupa lobata* Blainville. E.Afr. Brown bands, lobes, and columella. 1″ .75

37. *Drupa rubuscaesium* Röd. P.I. Cream and lavender about opening. 1¼″ .50

PLATE 2

Plate 3

1. *Astraea (Cookia) sulcata* Mart. N. Zeal. Top whorls greenish, body whorl brownish. Strong ridges curve across each whorl.
2″ 1.50

2. *Astraea aureola* Ired. Queensland, Aust. The glisten of pearl may show through the rough-textured gold of the surface. Gold color follows around the aperture to the pearled interior. Rare. 3″ 3.00 and up

3. *Astraea stellare* Gmel. Aust. White, circled by turned-up fluting. Base is yellowish near center, circling in sky blue to pearl interior. Sky blue operculum. 1½″ 1.25

4. *Tegula regina* Stearns. Calif. Dark rim winds down over-cream colored surface. Base is ribbed to look like a feather. Golden circle of umbilicus curved into pearled interior. Base 1⅞″ 2.75

5. *Turbo fluctuosus* Wood. W. Mex. A young shell, pearled. The species grow to about 2½″. 1″ .25

6. *Astraea phoebia* Röd. Fla. to W.I. Syn: *A. longispina* Lam. Young specimen exhibiting fine form. See also No. 19.
1″ 1.25

7. *Astraea brevispina* Lam. Fla. & W.I. Short-Spined Star. A flat, greenish-brown star. Edge with sawlike teeth. Pink near opening. Interior pearly. 1½″ 1.00

8. *Astraea tuber* L. Fla. to W.I. In shape of a top. Greenish with white showing through, giving a rough appearance although the shell itself and nodules are rounded and smooth. Flesh-colored about opening. Pearly interior. 2½″ 1.25

9. *Guildfordia yoca* Jousseaume. Japan. A copper-colored marvel. A fine shell even when all its fragile spines are not perfectly intact. Underneath white to pearly opening. Not common. Almost 2″ across whorls, 4″ across spines. 5.00

10. *Astraea brevispina* Lam. Jamaica. Short-Spined Star. Less flat than specimens described above. Pink to straw color. Perfect model for a lady's hat. 2½″ 2.00

11. *Angaria delphinus atrata* Reeve. Japan. Purple Dolphin. Circling purple lines. Dark tips of the sharp spines almost obscure the white ground. A dark, concave operculum sets off the pearly interior of a flaring, hexagonal aperture. 1½″ 1.00

12. *Astraea heliotropium* Mart. Aust. Heliotrope Star. Color faint heliotrope. Like other *Astreaidae* often roughened with lime incrustations and irregularly formed.
3″ 3.50, higher for unusual shells

13. *Astraea undosa* Wood. S. Calif. Waved Star. Larger specimens are rough, but when the epidermis is removed and the surface buffed, the pearl shell shows the waving edges and the beautifully rounded nodules.
5″ Natural 1.50, Polished 3.50

14. *Astraea imbricata* Gmel. W.I. Overlapping Star. White. Almost as high as it is wide. When lime is cleared away, it appears attractively spined. A touch of lilac about umbilicus and operculum. 2″ 1.25

15. *Astraea calcar* L. P.I. Mature specimen. White to yellowish brown. Yellow about the operculum and in the shell. 1¼″ .75

16. *Astraea calcar* L. P.I. Spurred Star. Immature specimen. Form differs from the mature shells (No. 15), but color about the same. 1¼″ .75

17. *Astraea buschii* Phil. W.Mex. White shows through green and brown ribs. All white below, with feathery cross-lines and heavy spiral rib. No red spot as in *Astraea olivacea* Wood, which this resembles closely. Not common. 1″ 1.25

18. *Astraea (Guilfordia) triumphans* Phil. Japan. Copper-colored, with fine spines. Pinkish line about the umbilicus merging into pearly interior.
1½″ body, 2″ across spines .75

19. *Astraea phoebia* Röd. Fla. to W.I. Syn: *A. longispina* Lam. White, trimmed with light green. Green at umbilicus. White inside. Large saw-toothed spines embroider each whorl and are curved up and back. See also No. 6. 2″ 2.00

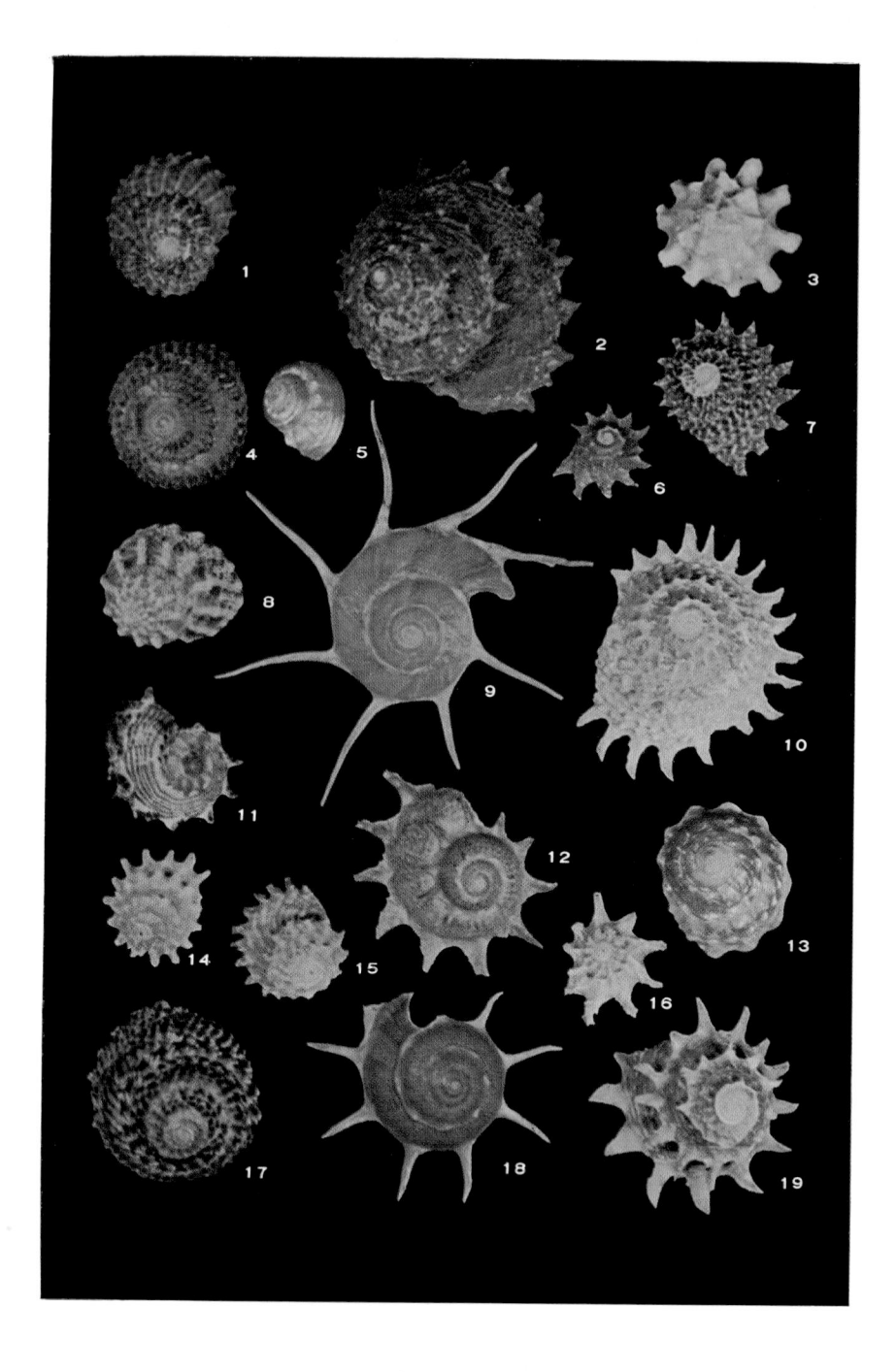

PLATE 3

Plate 4

1. *Strombus pugilis* L. W.I. Fighting Conch. A favorite because of the glossy, golden color of the body and aperture. For differences between *S. pugilis* L. and *S. alatus* Gmel., see Plate 33, Nos. 6 and 9.
3″ 1.00

2. *Strombus pipus* Röd. Indo-Pac. Syn: *S. papilio* "Chemnitz" Dillwyn. White with brown pattern. Purple-brown interior and dark bands on inner lip. Numerous pointed knobs. Not common. 2″ 1.50

3. *Strombus sinuatus* Humphrey. S.W.Pac. Syn: *S. laciniatus* "Chemnitz" Dillwyn. Aperture with peach deepening to brownish purple. Lacy edges extend over the square shoulder. 3½″ 1.75

4. *Lambis lambis* L. Indo-Pac. Shells of this genus were once called *Pterocera*. All of them have the winged look that the name suggests; all feature long, hooked canals varying in each species; and all have different, colored apertures. This one has an aperture flushed with peach and large knobs on a brown-patched body. Fine, large specimens have long curling hooks.
4″ 60, 6″ 1.50

5. *Lambis millipeda* L. S.W.Pac. About 12 hooks. Knobs on body whorl. Brown opening deepening inside to orange. Black and white lines growing out of the opening.
3½″ 1.25

6. *Lambis scorpio* L. Indo-Pac. Ornate. Dark brown to orange marking. Dark and light purple lines in aperture merging into orange at the edges. About 7 long arms with swollen nodules.
5″ With fine spines 2.50

7. *Lambis violacea* Swain. Mauritius. Distinctive spurs or spikes with stag-horn effect at top corners. Many ridges in the white aperture which deepens to violet. Rare.
3½″ 75.00 and up

8. *Lambis digitata* Perry. E.Afr. Syn: *L. elongata* Swain. Cream ground with coffee-colored markings making rings of raised nodules. About six short lacelike spurs with elongated spurs from the canal and two from the shoulders, one extending beyond the spire and branching like an antler. Yellow interior. Aperture with sharp black and white lines. Rare. 5″ 5.00 and up

9. *Conus archon* Brod. W.Mex. Magistrate Cone. Angular shoulder and sharp concave spire. White in aperture and body. Ringed with two heavily patched circles and one central lightly patched circle of irregular brown markings. 2¾″ 7.50 and up

10. *Conus circumactus* Ired. Indo-Pac. Syn: *C. pulchellus* Swain. Plump, with sloping spire patched with dark sickle moons. Four bands showing pink at shoulder, light brown, white, and then light brown. Tip of aperture is lavender. Rare. 2¼″ 6.50

11. *Conus adamsoni* Brod. Aust. Syn: *Conus rhododendron* Jay. White, marked with patches of pink-lavender. Narrow rings of brown dots. Very rare. This photo is a beach specimen.
2″ 15.00, Fine 75.00 and up

12. *Lambis chiragra arthritica* Röd. E.Afr. Differs from male *L. chiragra* L. by lacking deep-set long well at upper end of opening. White spiral lirae on parietal wall are not oblique but parallel with spiral cords. Aperture generally yellowish rose rather than pinkish rose. 4″—6″ 1.75

13. *Lambis crocata* Link. E.Afr. Saffron Scorpion. Syn: *Pterocera aurantia* Lam. With its golden aperture and slim curling hooks, this is deservedly a favorite.
5″ with spines perfect 1.75

14. *Tibia insulae-chorab* Röd. Red Sea. Syn: *T. curvirostris* Lam. Stockier than *Tibia fusus* L. and with stubby canal. Rare.
7″ 16.00 and up

15. *Tibia fusus* L. P.I. Famed Spindle Shell.
7″ 15.00 and up

PLATE 4

Plate 5

1. Cypraea hesitata Ired. N.S.W., Aust. One of the Australian cold water Wonder Cowries, usually dredged from deep water of 40 to 150 fms. Globose, but tapering toward the canal end. White base and white ground color showing through about the spots and on the dorsal line. Irregularly mottled with light brown. Definite umbilical depression. Uncommon. 3″ 3.75

2. Cypraea beddomei Schilder. N.S.W., Aust. A stunted form of *Cypraea hesitata* Ired., first reported by C. E. Beddome from New South Wales. 2″—2½″. 2½″ 5.00

3. Cypraea aurantia Gmel. Fiji & Pac. Is. Golden Cowry. This golden orange or peach-orange Cowry is one of the world's most coveted shells. The tips are pinkish white, merging into a white base. Strong orange teeth line the aperture. This is a royal shell, badge of a Fiji Chieftain, and is almost, but not quite, unobtainable. As demand increases, the price continues to rise. Rare. 3″—5″. Currently fresh caught about 3″ 150.00—175.00 and up

4. Cypraea carneola L. Indo-Pac. Carnelian Cowry. A handsome Cowry. Light brown with about four orange bands. The purple teeth distinguish it from the Golden Cowry with which large specimens are sometimes confused. About 2″, but there are giant specimens up to a little over 3″. 2″ 1.00

5. Cypraea hesitata howelli Ired. S.Aust. White form of *Cypraea hesitata* Ired. Usually caught in trawl nets from deep water. Rare. 3½″ 12.00

6. Cypraea stercoraria rattus Lam. W.Afr. This humpbacked Cowry has brown mottling on cream, merging into sides and base tinged with lavender to cream. The teeth form whitish ridges about the curving aperture. Regarded by some as a young form of *Cypraea stercoraria* L. Rare. 2¾″ 25.00 and up

7. Cypraea stercoraria L. W.Afr. Small brown dots against shades of brown to grey make this Cowry look a little like a fine bird's egg. The bottom is greyish, merging into brown about the grey toothed and curved lip. Wider at the canal end. 3″ 9.00

8. Cypraea scurra Gmel. Indo-Pac. Jester Cowry. Small and cylindrical, with definite dorsal line and spots against a network of small lines. Lower sides have black dots. This shell varies considerably and is sometimes prevailingly brown, sometimes bluegrey. 1½″ 2.25

9. Cypraea arabica immanis Schilder & Schilder. Indo-Pac. Arab Cowry. There are several shells in the *arabica* complex, a number being shown on this page. This one is covered with cream-brown hieroglyphic or vermiform lines against a cream background, assuming the form of lines and sprinkled dots. The dorsal line shows clearly. The side margins have bluish brown blotches, and the base is creamy fawn with brown teeth-lines. 3″ 1.25

10. Cypraea arabica histrio Gmel. Polynesia to Hawaii. Spotted with light circles or rhomboids. Dark spots on the whitish lower sides. Whitish base, almost free of dark spots. 2½″ 1.00

11. Cypraea maculifera Schilder. Indo-Pac. Spot-Bearing Cowry. High-backed member of the *arabica* complex, with cream-colored curved dorsal line and dots of cream against brownish lines. The lower sides appear callused with grey-purplish splotches which appear larger at the ends. Base shows a dark patch near the columellar teeth, of which there are about 24. On the outer lip are 24 to 34 teeth, broad, long, dark, and red-brown. Once this shell had the invalid name of *Cypraea reticulata* Mart. (non-binomial). See also Plate 6, No. 31. 2″ 1.00

12. Cypraea argus L. Indo-Pac. Eyed Cowry. Argus, the son of Zeus, had many eyes, some of which were always awake. The eyes scattered over the light brown of this cylindrical Cowry vary in size and in the thickness of the surrounding circles.

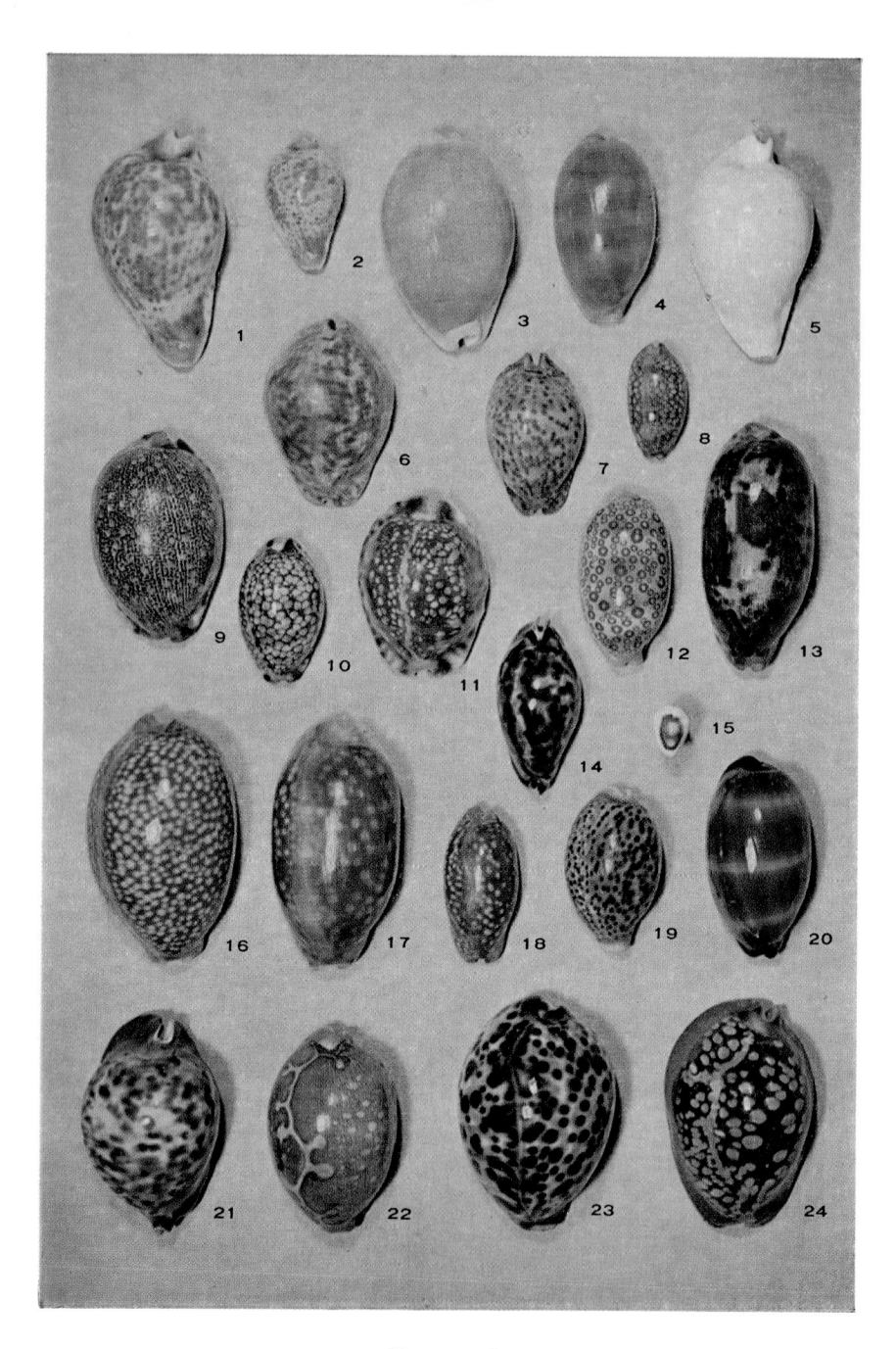

PLATE 5

Plate 5 (cont.)

Perhaps the most handsomely decorated of all the Cowries, this one has three brown bands on the fawn-colored background which extends on to the base with its two dark brown splotches on each lip and strong ribbed teeth. Not common.
2¼" 4.00

13. Cypraea testudinaria L. Indo-Pac. Tortoise Shell Cowry. The large size, combined with the cylindrical shape, make this Cowry unique. Lavish brown markings on light brown cause it to resemble tortoise shell. It is sprinkled with tiny white dots that look like dust. 4" 3.75

14. Cypraea friendi Gray. W.Aust. Syn: C. scotti Brod. This slim shell, richly mottled with brown, may show faint tinges of blue in the light cream background. Sides merge into deep brown below. Edges of the teeth show white in the aperture. A rare and beautiful Cowry much desired by collectors everywhere.
2¾" 12.00 and up

15. Cypraea moneta L. Indo-Pac. Money Cowry. This specimen has probably been treated with acid to reveal the underneath purple. It is used here as a color accent and to establish size relationship, since it is just over ¾" in size. The usually-yellow Money Cowry is described on another page. See Plate 6, Nos. 13 and 25.
¾" .25

16. Cypraea cervus L. N.C. to W.I. Stag Cowry or Micromac. Said to attain the largest size of any Cowry in the world. The best specimens come from 10 to 20 fms. It is shiny and globose, of a rich brown, with many cleanly cut, or at other times indistinct, unringed spots. Definite dorsal line. Plain base with strong brown teeth.
4" 4.00

17. Cypraea zebra L. N.C. to Fla. Measled Cowry. Syn: C. exanthema L. Often found on mangrove roots along the shore. This Cowry is fairly large and always has some light spots with dark centers near base. It is indistinctly banded, with a fawn-colored base and strong brown teeth. 3" 3.00

18. Cypraea cervinetta Kiener. W.Mex. Little Deer Cowry. Much like Cypraea cervus L. with light spots on brown, but a smaller shell which is more elongated and has darker teeth. 3½" 2.50

19. Cypraea pantherina Sol. Red Sea. Panther Cowry. Syns: C. vinosa Gmel. and C. tigrina Lam. Smaller and narrower than Cypraea tigris L. The sides are more vertical and the teeth more numerous. White to greyish and brownish, with many small dark spots. Base is white.
2½" 2.00

20. Cypraea talpa L. Indo-Pac. Mole Cowry. This glossy Cowry is regarded as one of the most handsome of them all. Specimens vary widely in the size of the wide or narrow bands of cream and dark brown. Lower tips, lower sides, and base are almost black about a narrow aperture with many linear teeth.
2½" 1.75

21. Cypraea thersites Gaskoin. S. Aust. A globelike shell. White, with rich brown mottling. Base of shell is white near the S-shaped aperture. Strong teeth. Some specimens are almost black. Uncommon.
3" 12.00

22. Cypraea mappa L. Indo-Pac. Map Cowry. The base color varies from fawn to reddish pink showing through top pattern of fine brown lines. One of the most handsome of the Cowries, this can be identified by the budlike branchings which make the dorsal line look like a delicate vein.
3" 3.00, pink base 6.00

23. Cypraea tigris L. Indo-Pac. Tiger Cowry. The size, color, form, and pattern of this universal favorite all vary widely. When it is colored at its best, the dark spotting is interwoven with touches of white, orange, red, blue, and green, any or all. A growth series is needed to see its changes from chestnut to whitish with interrupted bands and zig-zag brown flashes, to closely set wavy blotches, and later perhaps to a coat of white, and finally to the dark spots against complex mature color.
2" .20, 4" 2.00

Plate 5 (cont.)

24. *Cypraea mauritiana* L. Indo-Pac. Mauritius Cowry or Mourning Cowry. A stocky, humpbacked Cowry. Pink-brown spots and dorsal line on deep mahogany color. A "mourning" band of bluish black around the lower sides extends to cover the base. Curved aperture. Strong, dark brown teeth with white between. 3½″ 2.00

Plate 6

1. *Cypraea cylindrica* Born. Indo-Pac. Bluish grey, mottled finely with brown. Light brown patches at center and end. Faint bands. Base is faint pink. ⅞″ 1.00

2. *Cypraea lutea* Gmel. Indo-Pac. Brown, tipped with red and cut across with two thin lines of bluish white. Base is reddish with many black spots. ⅝″ 1.75

3. *Cypraea boivinii* Kiener. Pac. Over-all grey appearance. Small brown dots on white. Thin blackish line at tips and base. Outer lip is whitish. Dorsal line is bluish grey. ⅞″ 1.00

4. *Cypraea ursellus* Gmel. Indo-Pac. Swallow Cowry. Syns: *C. kieneri* Hidalgo and *C. hirundo* Sow. White background on tips and base, the white approximating two bands separating wide bands of grey-blue. Dark dots on white of lower sides. ½″ .60

5. *Cypraea zic-zac misella* Perry. E.Afr. Light brown, with bands of white zig-zags, like swallows in flight. Dark dots circling both ends and extending profusely into an orange base. ⅝″ 2.50

6. *Cypraea asellus* L. Indo-Pac. Porcelain white, with three shortened blackish bands. Used by primitive people as eyes for idols. ¾″ .75

7. *Cypraea labrolineata* Gaskoin. Indo-Pac. Light brown with tiny white dots. Faint dorsal line. Dark line near each tip and dots near edge of white base. ½″ 1.50

8. *Cypraea annulus* L. Indo-Pac. Ring Cowry. A flattened Cowry with a fine golden line. Pale blue-grey at the top within the line. Outside the line, flaring sides of cream color continuing over the plain base. 1″ 3 for .25

9. *Cypraea gaskoini* Reeve. Micronesia & Hawaii. Light yellow, with round white dots and dorsal line. White base. Rare. ⅝″ 16.00

10. *Cypraea helvola* L. Indo-Pac. Brown, with small white dots. Faint violet at tips and through dorsal line. Lower sides have a band of orange that runs over and across the base. ¾″ .60

11. *Cypraea arabicula* Lam. W.Mex. Little Arabian Cowry. Resembles the larger *Cypraea arabica*. Brown, with light dorsal line and mottling showing through. Lower sides are grey-blue with dots. Base is plain with faint color. ⅞″ 1.00

12. *Cypraea annulus obvelata* Lam. Indo-Pac. A flat Cowry with swollen, white to flesh-colored sides which enclose a bluish white raised center. Strong teeth. ⅞″ .50

13. *Cypraea moneta* L. Indo-Pac. See also No. 25. ¾″ .25

14. *Cypraea xanthodon* Sow. Aust. Yellowtooth. Pink base, but no yellow teeth, in spite of its name. Prevailingly greenish grey, with alternate light and darker bands, one mottled all over with dark dots. Dark dots on lower sides. Tips are pinkish. 1″ 1.00

15. *Trivia aperta* Swain. Open Trivia. Trivia used to be called Cowries and may still be loosely so called. This thin shell is seldom pictured but is shown in Reeve's monumental 19th-century *Conchologica Iconica* where it is named Wood Louse Cowry, *Cypraea oniscus* Lam. The wide pink globe of the shell is edged by ridges which run over the sides and across the base. Thin lip and wide aperture. See also Plate 8, No. 15. ¾″—1″. 1″ 1.00

16. *Cypraea cicercula* L. Pac. Chick Pea Cowry. Globose. Light brown with brown mottling and dark dots on sides. End drawn out. A small groove at posterior ends of dorsum. ⅝″ 1.00

17. *Cypraea ziczac diluculum* Reeve. E.Afr. Daybreak Cowry. Syn: *C. undata* Lam. White base and background, with brown marking in solid and waving bands which vary extensively from shell to shell. A line of dark at both ends. ⅝″ 1.00

18. *Trivia radians* Lam. W.Mex. to Ecuador. Beige to pink. Flat-shaped, with darkened nodules on each side of the mid-

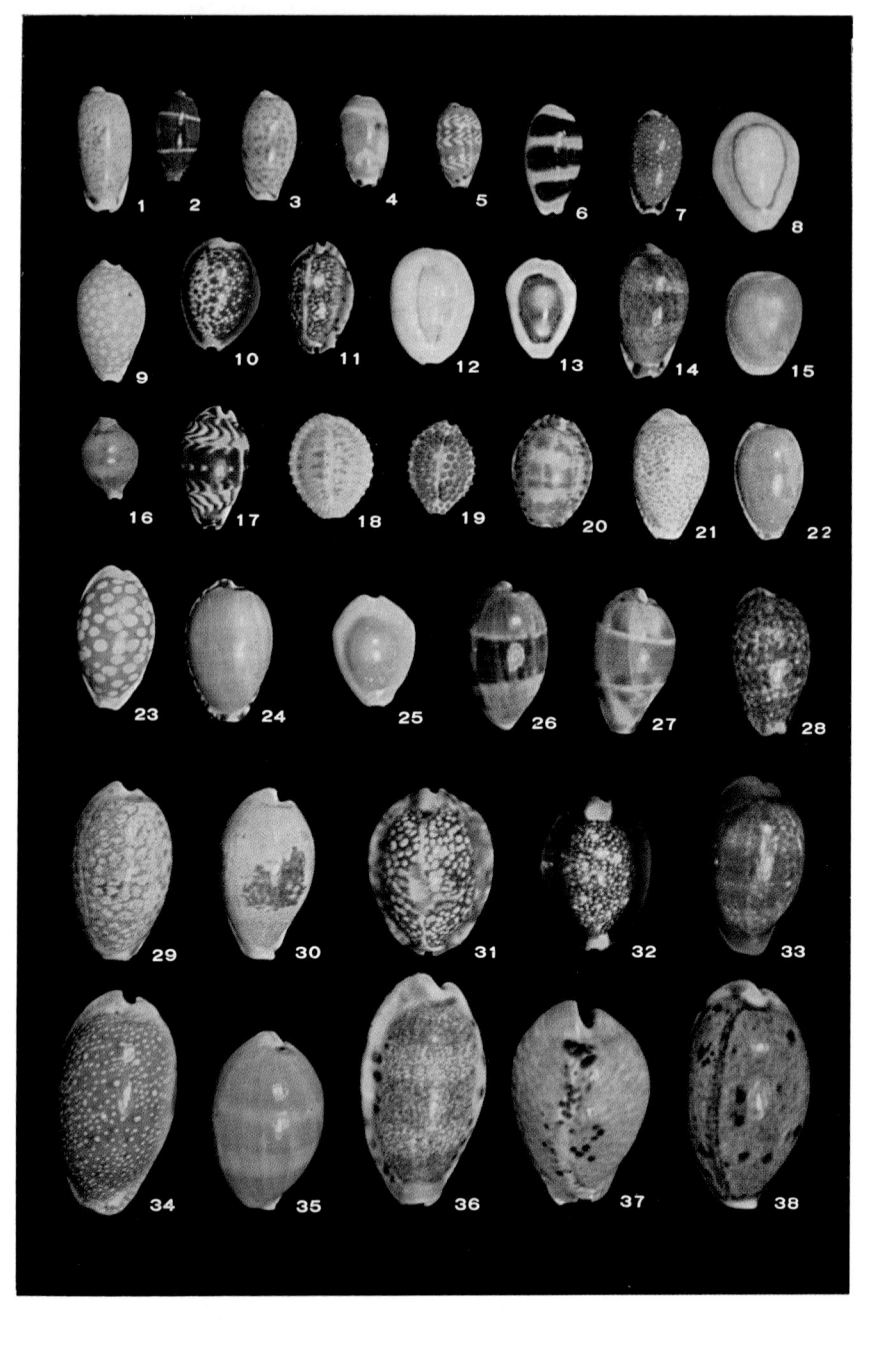

PLATE 6

Plate 6 (cont.)

dorsal line. Ribs on flattened edges about the dorsum look like a frill. Strong ribs across the base. ⅞" .50

19. *Jenneria pustulata* Sol. W.Nicaragua. Thoroughly distinctive with its blue mid-dorsal line and coverage of small red pustules. Base is brown, crossed with thin whitish ribs. Interior is purple. ¾" 1.25

20. *Cypraea robertsi* Hidalgo. W.Mex. to Peru. Faint blue ground crossed by indefinite brown bands. Flare of sides in bands of salmon color to light inky blue with dark dots. Base is cream. Teeth show sharply against purple interior. 1" .75

21. *Cypraea turdus* Lam. Ind.Oc. Thrush Cowry. Cream-colored with many light brown dots. White base. 1" 1.25

22. *Cypraea walkeri comptoni* Gray. Aust. Authorities are in disagreement about this race, but the name *comptoni* Gray survives. Light brown with indistinct light brown bands. Dark dots on lower sides. Base is white. 1" 1.50

23. *Cypraea cribraria* L. Indo-Pac. Sieve Cowry. Elongated. Unmistakably marked. Light brown ground which shows off the white circles and the white edge of the turned-up lip margin. White base. 1" 2.75

24. *Cypraea verconis* Cotton & Godfrey. S.E.Aust. Once regarded as *Cypraea angustata* Gmel. Light brown, almost pinkish. Plain dorsum. Upturned margin on one side and anterior end showing brown dots which appear on lower sides. Base is white. Wide aperture. 1" 2.00

25. *Cypraea moneta* L. Indo-Pac. Money Cowry. A real beauty that looks like gold and countless tons of which have been used for money over much of the world for unknown numbers of centuries. Young shells are pale cream, with three yellow bands. Mature specimens may have a greenish yellow dorsum and vary in color from creamy yellow to shades of deep orange. The raised central portion looks like a jewel for which the wide low margin forms a setting. See also No. 13. ¾" .25

26. *Cypraea walkeri surabajensis* Schilder.

Indo-Pac. Two converging blue-grey lines divide the dorsum into a dark brown central band and two greyish brown end bands. Base has some dark dots on a richly colored mixture of salmon to orange-brown, with purple staining about teeth and interior. Uncommon. 1" .75

27. *Cypraea walkeri continens* Ired. Aust. Two light brown converging cross-lines divide this pear-shaped shell into three brown mottled bands, the mid-band being the darkest. Dark brown dots on the light brown of lower sides. Light brown base and teeth. Rare. 1¼" 2.50

28. *Cypraea annettae* Dall. W.Mex. Annette's Cowry. Rich brown mottling on lighter brown forms traces of banding. Lower sides have round dots on light brown which continues on plain base. Purplish within wide aperture. 1⅛" .75

29. *Cypraea chinensis* Gmel. Indo-Pac. Marking often pale, but when stronger, appears as a network of very light brown spots and dorsal line on light brown. Lower sides dotted with purplish spots. White teeth with orange interstices. 1½" 1.00

30. *Cypraea subviridis* Reeve. Aust. Faintly greenish. Three bands, the central one lighter and blotched with brown. Tips are pinkish. Pear-shaped. Umbilicated at the spire. Base is white. Inner lip is orange. 1¼" 1.50

31. *Cypraea maculifera* Schilder. Hawaii. White line and dots show through brown reticulations. Margin flaring with inky blotches on white. Dark blotch on base. Strong brown teeth. See also Plate 5, No. 11. 2" 1.00

32. *Cypraea caputserpentis* L. Indo-Pac. Serpent's Head. White dots and end patches show through brown reticulations and brown band sloping toward the margins. 1¼" .25

33. *Cypraea pyrum* Gmel. S.Europe on Med. Sea. Pear Cowry. Cream color showing through dark brown mottling and banding. Sides darker toward the base with faint spots. Tips and base are orange-red. White teeth. 1½" 2.50

34. *Cypraea erosa* L. Indo-Pac. Eroded Cowry. Pale blue to yellowish brown,

Plate 6 (cont.)

snowed over with round dots giving effect of erosion. Margin and ends are faint pink to cream. A squarish patch where margin of each lip joins cream-colored base. Strong teeth extend to margin of outer lip.
1″—1¾″ .30—.60

35. *Cypraea cinerea* Gmel. W.I. Ashen Cowry. Swollen light brown to greyish Cowry. Thin bands of blue-grey cross the brownish shell. White base. 1″ 1.00

36. *Cypraea caurica* L. Indo-Pac. Thick-Edged Cowry. Stocky. Light and darker brown bands, finely mottled. Callused margins are pinkish with a few purple-brown spots. Plain base and strong teeth. There are several varieties of *caurica*, as it ranges from the Philippines to East Africa.
1¾″ .50

37. *Cypraea mus* L. Venezuela. Mouse Cowry. A wide, high shell. Pinkish ground covered with small mottling of light brown. Dark brown spots are sprinkled irregularly on both sides of the dorsal line. Aperture wide, inner lip small, and teeth few. Teeth on outer lip are tipped with orange-brown and produced across the wide lip perhaps even beyond the margin. Recently very scarce. 1¾″ 15.00 and up

38. *Cypraea lynx* L. Indo-Pac. Lynx Cowry. A beautiful color tapestry, basically grey-blue, but with orange-brown dorsal line, the same color staining part of the mottling. A sprinkling of dark dots with indefinite edges. White base ornamented by orange-red between the long teeth.
1¼″—2″ .15—.40

Plate 7

1. *Cypraea spadicea* Swain. Calif. Chestnut Cowry. Rich brown edged by pale lavender. White base. 1¾″ 1.00

2. *Cypraea eglantina niger* Roberts. New Caledonia. Dark brown, with cream dorsal line and ends. Cream base perhaps shaded with orange. 1¾″ 30.00 and up

3. *Cypraea ventriculus* Lam. Pac. Top of back is variable rich brown with the wide "window" showing white and carnelian bands. Sides are smoky, with fine descending lines. Faint salmon base. 1¾″ 1.25

4. *Cypraea lamarcki* Gray. Ind.Oc. Yellow-brown varying to orange or greenish with white dots. Light dorsal line. Reddish brown dots on lower sides becoming lines at ends. White base. Strong teeth. 1¼″ 1.00

5. *Cypraea onyx adusta* Lam. E.Afr. Slim, shiny, pear-shaped beauty. Its deep coffee-brown turns almost to black on edges and base. Uncommon. 1½″ 2.75

6. *Cypraea pulchella* Swain. China & Indo-Pac. Pear-shaped, umbilicate, with elongated patches of orange-red and marginal dots and teeth the same color. Rare. 1½″ 9.50

7. *Cypraea vitellus* L. Indo-Pac. Calf Cowry. Plump. Flecked with round white dots on ash to greyed yellow. Sides with lines over whitish base to teeth. 1½″ .40

8. *Cypraea sanguinolenta* Gmel. W.Afr. Shiny, ashy purple, with brown cloud and dots, distinguishing purplish dots on sides, and possibly a smoky patch on pinkish base. Rare. ¾″ 10.00

9. *Cypraea teulerei* Cazenavette. Persian Gulf. White Mouth Cowry. Syn: C. *leucostoma* Gaskoin. Greyish, with brown patch and dots and unique dorsal line usually forked at ends. Base is white. Rare. 1¾″ 65.00 and up

10. *Cypraea pulchra* Gray. Red Sea. Shiny buff brown. Lightly banded. At each end are dark patches like eyes. Base is pinkish to white. Rare. 1½″ 10.00

11. *Cypraea onyx* L. Indo-Pac. Onyx Cowry. Superb in a series since dorsum shows different variable patterns of cloudy whitish blue and of bands showing white patches. Brown dorsal stripes and brown edges. Black base. 1½″ 1.00

12. *Cypraea lurida* L. Italy. Shining grey-brown, with two dark spots at each end. Base is white and teeth short. 1¼″ 2.25

13. *Cypraea reevei* Sow. S.W.Aust. Thin, globose, and pinkish brown. Lightly banded and shiny. Single dark dot at each pinkish tip. Rare. 1½″ 12.00 and up

14. *Cypraea cylindrica* Born. N.W.Aust. Bluish, with greyish banding on a large brown dorsal patch and dots. Two dark dots at each end. Base is grey. Lip and side are white. ⅞″ 1.00

15. *Cypraea sulcidentata* Gray. Hawaii. Groove-Toothed Cowry. Broad and stocky, white or darker, with brown bands on lighter brown. Long deep-cut teeth across a flesh-colored to smoky base which slopes away toward dorsum. 1½″ 10.00 and up

16. *Cypraea decipiens* E. A. Smith. N.W. Aust. Chubby and humped. Rich brown with small patches and dorsal line of cream. Base is deep orange and brown. Scarce. 1¾″ 4.00 and up

17. *Cypraea schilderorum* Ired. Pac. Sandy Cowry. Syn: C. *arenosa* Gray. Stocky and wide. Fine pale shades. Several bands of orange-brown, all ringed at the margins with smoky brown. Base is white. Short teeth. 1⅜″ 2.75

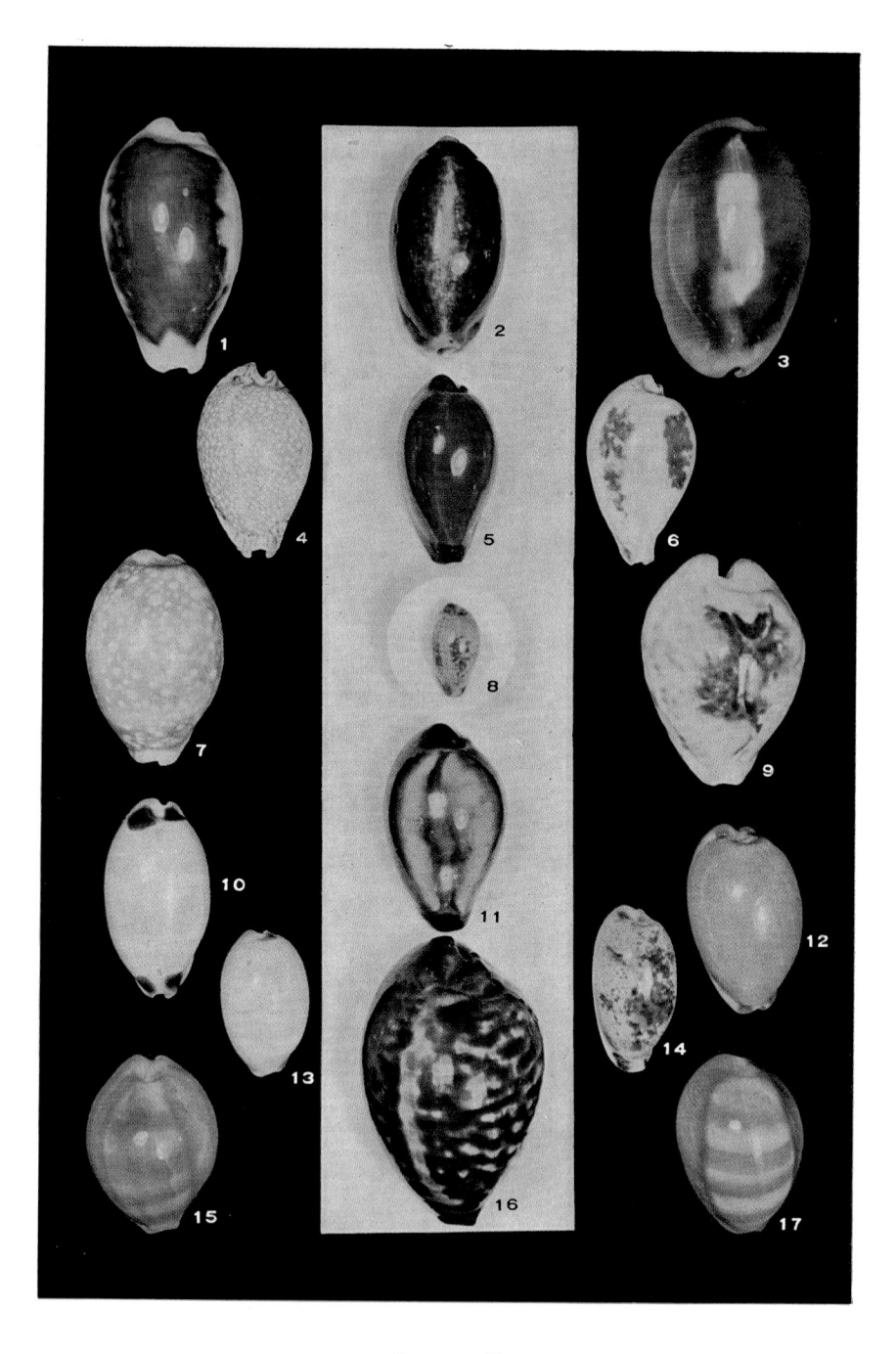

PLATE 7

Plate 8

1. *Cypraea quadrimaculata* Gray. N.W. Aust. Minute flecks of light brown on blue-grey. Two brown dots at each end. Margin and base are white. 3/4″ 2.50

2. *Cypraea microdon* Gray. Indo-Pac. Oblong, banded ovate. Minute teeth. See also No. 13. 1/2″ 3.00

3. *Trivia ovulata* Lam. S.Afr. Globular, smooth, and rose-colored. Whitish margin, lip, and base. Faint inner teeth and strong outer ones. 3/4″ 1.00

4. *Cypraea coxeni* Cox. Papua. Unusual appearance. Translucent cream-white base, margins, and background. Dorsum with interlacing dark brown mottling. Rare. 1″ 1.50

5. *Cypraea clandestina passerina* Melvill. E.Afr. Banded in faint zig-zag brown hair lines over light to darker lilac-grey. Pale orange ends. Sides and base are white. 1/2″—3/4″. 3/4″ .60

6. *Cypraea fimbriata durbanensis* Schilder & Schilder. Mozambique. Flat broad ends and flat base. End dots are violet-brown. Whitish. Mottled and banded in brown and grey. About 5/8″ 1.00

7. *Cypraea teres* Gmel., 1791. E.Afr. Syn: *C. tabescens* Dillwyn, 1817. See also No. 28. White or shaded with colors. Bands of brown mottling. Dots on raised margin. Ends produced. 1 1/4″ 1.25

8. *Volva birostris* L. S.Afr. One of the Spindle Cowries. Reddish. 1″ 1.00

9. *Cypraea goodalli goodalli* Sow. Pac. White, with orange-brown patches or bands. Rare. 3/8″ 2.50

10. *Cypraea poraria scarabaeus* Bory. Cent. Pac. Brown, with fine dots of pinkish violet on edges and dorsum. See No. 11 for aperture side. 5/8″ .75

11. *Cypraea poraria scarabaeus* Bory. Cent. Pac. Aperture side. For dorsal side, see No. 10. 5/8″ .75

12. *Cypraea dillwyni* Schilder. Polynesia. Yellow, with white spots. Very fine teeth on outer lip. White base. 1/2″ 2.50

13. *Cypraea microdon* Gray. Polynesia. Syn: *C. serrulifera* Schilder & Schilder. Pale blue or fulvous. Faint bands and lilac tips. White base. About 32 teeth on inner lip, and 24 on outer. See also No. 2. 1/2″ 3.00

14. *Cypraea felina* Gmel. Indo-Pac. Cat Cowry. Finely mottled greenish blue, with perhaps small patches of orange. Edges and base are cream-orange, and lower sides have dark purple-brown dots. 3/4″ .75

15. *Trivia aperta* Swain. S.Afr. Wood Louse Cowry. Syn: *Trivia oniscus* Lam. Pinkish or brownish, inflated, and wrinkled over white edge and base. See also Plate 6, No. 15. 3/4″ 1.00

16. *Cypraea eburnea* Barnes. Fiji. Ivory Cowry. Pear-shaped. Pure white, with crinkled edges. 1 1/2″ 2.00

17. *Cypraea coloba* Melvill. Mauritius. Pinkish, with scattered light brown dots. Flat bulging margins. Coarse teeth, middle ones shorter. 3/4″ 5.00

18. *Cypraea edentula* Gray. S.Afr. Toothless Cowry. Light brown, with darker mottling. Ends and margin are extended and white. Back and base are slightly flat. Teeth are vestigial. 1″ 1.00

19. *Cypraea tessellata* Swain. Hawaii. Yellow-brown back. Three bands. Squarish, brown and white spots on sides. Dark chestnut spots on both sides. This is a semi-fossil form. Scarce. 1 1/4″ 12.00, rare live-caught 40.00

20. *Cypraea achatidea* Sow. Algiers. Syn: *C. physis* Deshayes. Pear-shaped. Cream, with generous number of brown spots and bands. Salmon margin paling to smooth white base. 1 1/4″ 5.00

21. *Cypraea hirasei* Roberts. Japan. Pear-shaped. Pink to flesh at margins. Brown mottling and netting. Ends extended. White base. Rare. 1 1/2″ 45.00 and up.

22. *Cypraea hungerfordi* Sow. Japan. Solid and pear-shaped. White background under orange stippling. Side dots high on a white band which merges into salmon edges, ends and base. 1 1/2″ 3.00

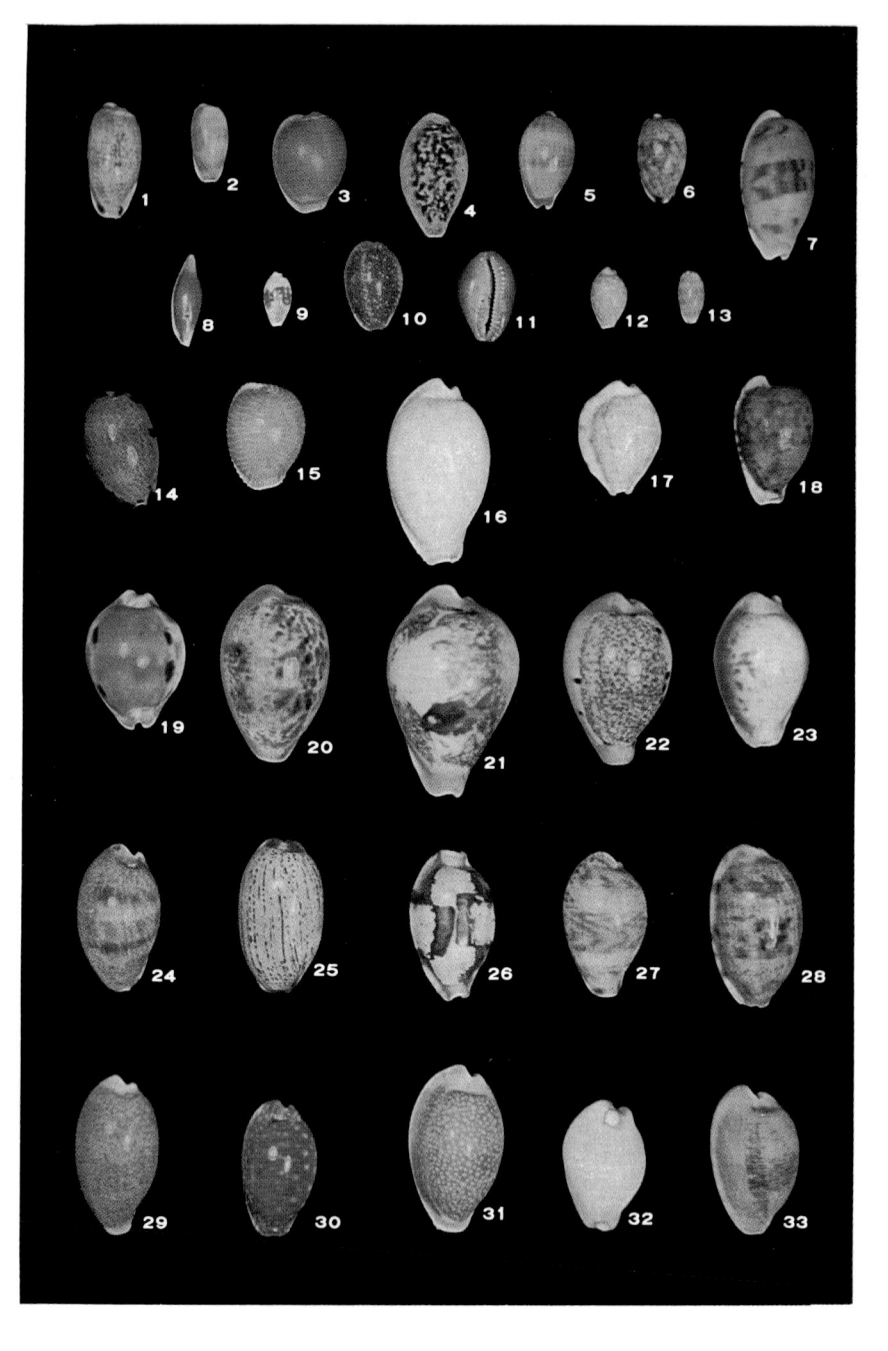

PLATE 8

Plate 8 (cont.)

23. *Cypraea surinamensis* **Perry,** 1811. Lesser Antilles. Syn: *C. bicallosa* Gray, 1831. Faint pink, with saffron edges and base. End-calluses. Strong teeth. Very rare. 1¼" 120.00

24. *Cypraea nigropunctata* Gray. Galapagos. Black Spotted Cowry. Bluish, freckled with reddish brown. Black dots on side. Yellowish base. Sharply cut teeth. Rare. 1" 6.00

25. *Cypraea isabella* L. Indo-Pac. Cylindrical. Fawn grey, with long, dark, interrupted lines. Orange tips. White base. 1¼" .50

26. *Cypraea stolida* L. Indo-Pac. Stolid Cowry. Pale blue or cream. If well marked, has brown mottlings in checkered effect. Strong teeth to margin. 1⅛" 6.00 and up

27. *Cypraea lentiginosa* Gray. Ceylon. Whitish, with light brown dots and wavy bands. Dots over white base. Teeth are distant. A juvenile here. 1" 15.00

28. *Cypraea teres* Gmel., 1791. Indo-Pac. Syn: *C. tabescens* Dillwyn, 1817. See also No. 7. Faint pink with mottled brown banding. Pale purplish dots on swollen pink edge. Base is white. 1¼" 1.25

29. *Cypraea errones* L. Pac. Color varies, perhaps cream or grey, with fine olive-brown marks and a trace of banding. White base. ¾"—1¼". 1" .50

30. *Cypraea facifer* Iredale. N. Queensland, Aust. Fawn, with white dots, orange ends, and marginal pitting. Base is white. Strong teeth. 1" 1.00

31. *Cypraea miliaris* Gmel., Pac. Millet Cowry. Mustard color, with snowstorm of dots. Margins and base are white. 1"—1¼". 1" .50

32. *Calpurnus verrucosus* L. Indo-Pac. Warted Egg Shell. Allied to Cowries, this favorite paper-white shell has a crease, forming a hump, and a tubercle at end. 1" .50

33. *Cypraea capensis* Gray. S.Afr. Cape Cowry. Pinkish to brown circle with fine sculptured lines on top and base. Central mottling. 1" Beach 1.25

Plate 9

1. *Cymatium cynocephalus* Lam. E.Afr. Syn: *C. cingulata* Lam. When in W.I. *C. caribbaeum* Clench and Turner. Brown, with one varix. Aperture enameled salmon, dark-stained inside at columella. Canal bent back. 3" 1.50

2. *Cymatium gemmifera* Euthyme. S.Afr. Syn: *C poecilostoma* E. A. Smith. Brown. White on columella and inside. Brown bands on lip. 3" 1.25

3. *Cymatium nicobaricum* Röd. Pac. Syn: *C. chlorostoma* Lam. Varices, circling lines nodulous. Seven paired teeth inside lip. Canal short, recurved. 3" 1.00

4. *Cymatium pileare* L. Fla. to Brazil to Indo-Pac. Close spiral ribs crossed by axial lines. Dark bands on varices. Teeth on lip become raised, entering lines. Lines on columella. Interior stained brown to blood red. Canal is short and recurved. 3" Fine color 1.00

5. *Cymatium grandimaculatum* Reeve. Indo-Pac. Orange-brown, rugged, and twisted. Dark bands on varices and lip, and blotches above columella. Single denticle near upper notch of opening. Swellings inside edge of lip. 2¾" 2.00

6. *Cymatium echo* Kuroda et Habe. Japan. Brown and nodulous. Six bifurcated, white-on-black teeth on lip. Columella with white lines on black. One raised darkly marked varix at beginning of each whorl. 3½" .75

7. *Cymatium (Charonia) tritonis* L. Indo-Pac. Triton or Trumpet Shell. Syn: *Triton tritonis* L. One of the world's favorite and most famous shells. Used from time immemorial in folk ceremonies. Small

PLATE 9

Plate 9 (cont.)

specimens appear gemmed. Huge shells are magnificent. Shiny body whorl is sumptuously curved. Spire high and tapering. Tip almost always broken. The scalloped pattern of white, light and dark brown, and perhaps a touch of blue-grey is superb. Orange inside opening. Sharp teeth on lip. Purplish at apex. Pattern is remarkable, but scarcely describable. Specimen shown 8″.
8″ 6.00, 15″ 12.00 and up

8. *Cymatium dunkeri* Lisch. Japan. Brownish axial ribs with nodules. White callus over opening. Lip channels inward. White inside. Canal bent back. 4″ 2.00

9. *Cymatium caudatum* Gmel. P.I. Cream color with thin, brown axial lines. Orange-brown enamel on opening. Seven orange teeth in lip. Canal is long. 2¼″ 2.75

10. *Cymatium variegata* Lam. Fla. & W.I. Syn: *C. nobilis* Conrad. A West Indies species which might be considered a variety of *C. tritonis*. The specimen photographed shows rich blue-grey and chocolate markings. Sometimes the shoulder is swollen, giving the illusion that the upper whorls are bent. Size seems generally to be smaller than the Pacific species. This specimen 6″.
6″ 4.50

11. *Cymatium spengleri* Perry. Aust. Cream, circled with close nodulose ridges with brown between them. White inside.
3″ 1.50

12. *Cymatium pyrum* L. Pac. Bright reddish orange is characteristic. White inner teeth and white lines on columella. 3″ 2.00

13. *Cymatium lotorium* L. P.I. Orange-brown. Unmistakable due to rows of three nodules on body whorl. Twisted appearance. Dark marks about aperture. White inner teeth. This specimen is 5″. 4″ 2.25

Plate 10

1. *Murex bednalli* Brazier. E.Aust. White, usually with orange markings. Three wide wings. Small aperture. Inner and outer teeth in lip. See also No. 2.
2⅞″ 35.00 and up

2. *Murex bednalli* Brazier. N.W.Aust. Rare color form of No. 1. 2½″ 50.00 and up

3. *Murex maurus sauliae* Sow. P.I. Brown, with rich foliation and fronds tipped with pink. Teeth on outer lip. Lack of teeth on columella and presence of short intermediate fronds on lip distinguish this from *M. palma-rosea* Lam. Rare. 3″ 7.00

4. *Murex trialatus* Sow. S.Calif. Three thick, rounded, wing-like varices, often turned backward. 2¼″ 2.50

5. *Murex palma-rosea* Lam. Indo-Pac. Slim brown shell. Highly frondose. Ends of the fronds are whitish, pinkish only in some specimens. Distinguished by presence of teeth on the columella in addition to those on lip. No short intermediate fronds on lip. Inside is white. 4″ 10.00

6. *Murex antillarum* Hinds. E.Mex. to Cuba. Antilles Murex. Rich brown on orange. Long, sharp, curved spines.
2¾″ 5.00

7. *Murex recurvirostris sallasi* R. & A. Yucatan, E.Mex. Light brown, with brown bands. Delicate form. Short stout spines at outward corners. 1¾″ 7.00

8. *Murex cailleti* Petit. Fla. & W.I. Plump white shell, with thick rounded varices and small nodules. Short spines. 1½″ 3.50

9. *Murex pulcher* A. Adams. Dominica. Syn: *M. consuela* H. Verrill. Brown markings on cream. Elongated, with long varices and sharp nodules. Long curved canal is characteristic. 2¼″ 10.00

10. *Murex tripterus* Born. P.I. White, with a yellowish inside. Wide wings. Teeth on lip. Filigree on body and wings.
2″ 15.00

11. *Murex triformis* Reeve. S.Aust. Brown, with three triangular sides separated by flat wings. Notch rounded into corner of flaring lip. 2″ 1.25

PLATE 10

Plate 11

1. *Ancilla elongata* Gray. N.W.Aust. Thin and translucent. White. Brown near top. 1¼″ 1.00

2. *Ancilla fulma* Swainson. Red Sea. Light yellow, with edging of pink-orange. Scarce. 1¼″ 1.50

3. *Ancilla tankervillei* Sow. Venezuela. Shiny yellow, shaded and banded at ends with pink-orange. Scarce. 2″—2¼″. 2″ 2.50

4. *Ancilla albocallosa* Lisch. Japan. Body is pinkish. Ends banded in brown. White callus on spire end of aperture side. 2¼″ 1.35

5. *Ancilla apicalis* Taki. Japan. Blue-grey, with descending lines. Chocolate bands near both ends. Not common. 1¾″ 1.50

6. *Ancilla optima* Sow. Natal. Body banded so half brown and half cream. Callus on aperture side is brown and white. One shown here *ex pisce*. Rare. 2″ 2.50

7. *Ancilla velesiana* Ired. N.S.W., Aust. Thin and shiny. Body is light brown. Ends have narrow white on broad brown bands. 3½″ 3.00

8. *Ancilla albozonata* Sow. S.Afr. White, with orange streaks on body and orange ring on spire. ¾″ .50

9. *Ancilla balteata niveus* Sow. Moluccas. Polished yellow to cream. Smooth form. 1″—1½″. 1¼″ 1.00

10. *Ancilla torosa* Meusch. Mauritius. Typical wide light and dark bands of the genus, but spire rounded like a finger end. Scarce. 1¼″ 1.50

11. *Ancilla mucronata* Sow. N. Zeal. Body is brown to pinkish. Ends are orange-brown. Callus-like spire. Scarce. 1¼″ 1.00

12. *Harpa harpa* L. P.I. Syn: *H. nobilis* Rumphius. Harp form, with handsome tapestry of color in white, brown, and red. Crescent marking between the slightly pleated ribs. Black lines across ribs. See also No. 13. 2½″ 2.50

13. *Harpa harpa* L. P.I. Syn: *H. nobilis* Rumphius. Aperture side. Dark brown patches on the columella. Black lines at edge of lip. See also No. 12. 2½″ 2.50

14. *Harpa doris* Röd. W.Afr. Syn: *H. rosea* Lam. Light, with high spire, rose-and-white-colored scallops, and rose bands across ribs. 2½″ 20.00 and up

15. *Ancilla contusa* Reeve. Natal. This specimen *ex pisce*. Smooth body and spire. Brown band at middle and end. Brown stain across columella. Rare. 1¾″ 2.00

16. *Harpa amouretta* Röd. Indo-Pac. Syn: *H. minor* Lam. Faint brown markings and lines on slightly pleated ribs. Faint scalloping between ribs. Elongated. 2″ .75

17. *Harpa major* Röd. Indo-Pac. Aperture side. Shows two patches of deep brown enamelling. See also No. 20. 3″ 2.00

18. *Harpa davidis* Röd. Indo-Pac. Syn: *H. conoidalis* Lam. Light to dark markings. Slightly pleated ribs tend to be narrow with dark cross-lines. Distinguished by single large blotch on columella. Startling and fine color occurs in this and other Harps. See also No. 21. 3″ 2.50

19. *Harpa articularis* Lam. P.I. There is as yet no authoritative naming for some Harps. This often has pale rose coloration and few, narrow, somewhat pleated ribs. 2½″ 1.50

20. *Harpa major* Röd. Indo-Pac. Syn: *H. ventricosa* Lam. A magnificent Harp, with clear banding and scalloping in brown, through pink, to white. Ribs characteristically wide and strongly pleated. See also No. 17. 3″ 2.00

21. *Harpa davidis* Röd. Indo-Pac. Aperture side. Shows large distinguishing dark blotch. See also No. 18. 3″ 2.50

22. *Harpa crenata* Swainson. W.Mex. Only American Harp. Tends to pale color in ribs and scallops. Ribs with descending broken line but not pleated. Often some small dark blotches. Variable blotching on columella. Not common. 1¾″—3½″. 3¼″ 3.00

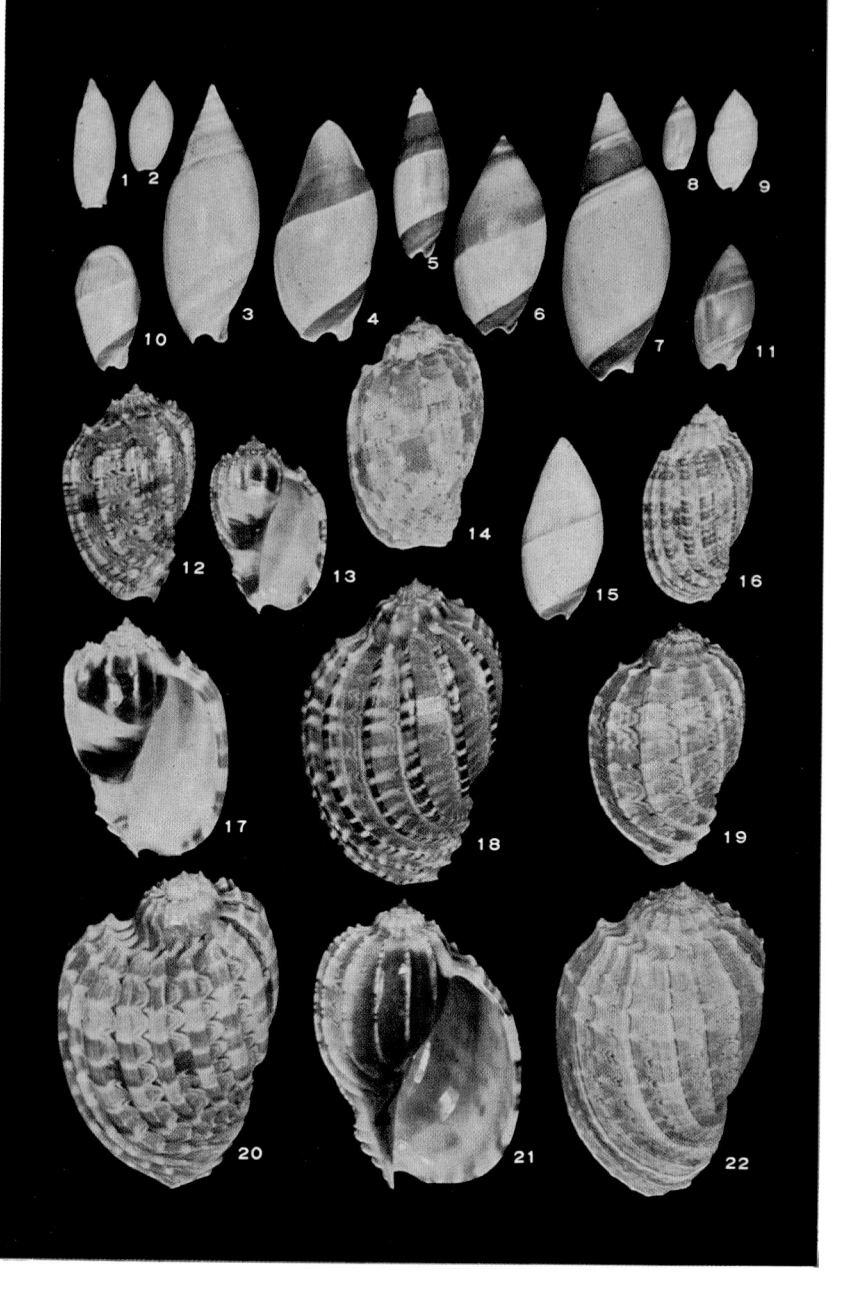

PLATE 11

Plate 12

1. *Oliva funebralis* Lam. Aust. White. Bluish or chocolate inside. 1½″ .60

2. *Oliva rufula* Ducl. P.I. Obliquely banded in brown. 1¼″ 1.75

3. *Oliva spicata polpasta* Ducl. Panamic Prov. Brown spots. White triangle below suture. 1½″ .60

4. *Oliva fuscata* Marrat. Gulf of Calif. Marks hidden by brown layer. Terminology unsettled. Possibly variety of *O. spicata*. 1½″ .50

5. *Oliva carneola* Gmel. P.I. Purple or orange marks. Spire callused. 1″ .50

6. *Oliva ispidula* L. P.I. Many ash to brown variations. See also No. 13. 1¼″ .25

7. *Agaronia testacea* Lam. W.Mex. Ashy. Pointed, with a wide opening. 2″ .50

8. *Oliva mustellina* Lam. P.I. Brown zig-zags. Violet inside. 1¼″ .30

9. *Oliva elegans* Lam. P.I. Brown, with cloudy zig-zags. 1½″ .50

10. *Oliva trujilloi* Clench. Dominica. Stocky. Lip is thick. Brown flecks in two faint bands. 1½″ .50

11. *Oliva oliva* L. P.I. Syns: *O. cincta* Dautz. and *O. maura* Lam. Faint dark bands on red-brown. Red tip. See also No. 32. 2″ .50

12. *Oliva tremulina* Lam. P.I. Yellowish. Brown axial waves and three dark bands. 2″ 1.00

13. *Oliva ispidula* L. P.I. Variation of No. 6. 1¼″ .25

14. *Ancilla australis* Sow. N. Zeal. Blue into brown. Pale callus on spire. 1″ .50

15. *Oliva marmorea* Mart. Cape Verde Is. Brown marbling on white. Many plaits. 1⅛″ 2.00

16. *Oliva annulata* Gmel. P.I. Syn: *O. emicator carnicolor* Dautz. Pink variety. Terminology unsettled. See also No. 24. 2″ 1.00

17. *Oliva australis* Ducl. Aust. This specimen pale. Usually whitish purple. 1″ .50

18. *Olivella volutella* Lam. W.Panama. Variations are white, blue, purple, brown, or mixed. 1″ .25

19. *Agaronia propatula* Conrad. Panamic Prov. Syn: *A. hiatula* Gmel. Ash grey axial lines. Purplish inside. 1¼″ .25

20. *Oliva sanguinolenta* Lam. P.I. Syn: *O. variabilis* Röd. Grey, mottled, and banded. End is red. 1½″ .35

21. *Oliva erythrostoma marrati* Johnson. P.I. Dark brown form. See also No. .45 3″ 1.25

22. *Oliva peruviana fulgurata* Martens. Peru. Cream. Zig-zagging brown axial lines. 1¾″ 1.00

23. *Oliva ornata* Marrat. Aust. Brown bands and faint zig-zags. 1½″ .75

24. *Oliva annulata* Gmel. Indo-Pac. Syn: *O. emicator* Meusch. Cream. Bluish spots and orange inside. See also No. 16. 1½″ .50

25. *Oliva sanguinolenta evania* Ducl. P.I. Mottling in light and dark bands. End is red. 1½″ .50

26. *Oliva ornata cryptospira* Ford. P.I. Brownish zig-zags showing through orange overlay. Inside is white. 2″ 1.00

27. *Oliva spicata* Röd. W.Mex. Buff, with brown marks. High spire. 1½″ .35

28. *Oliva splendidula* Sow. Panamic Prov. Cream, with two bands of brown dots and triangles. Not common. 1½″ 1.25

29. *Oliva episcopalis* Lam. Indo-Pac. Black specks and spots, sometimes in an upper and mid-band. Purple aperture. 1¾″ .75.

30. *Oliva reticularis* Lam. W.I. Brown zig-zagging axial lines on white. 1½″ .35

31. *Oliva bulbosa* Röd. E.Afr. Syn: *O. inflata* Lam. Exceedingly variable. A series would show lovely patterns of white through brown and black. 1¼″ .30

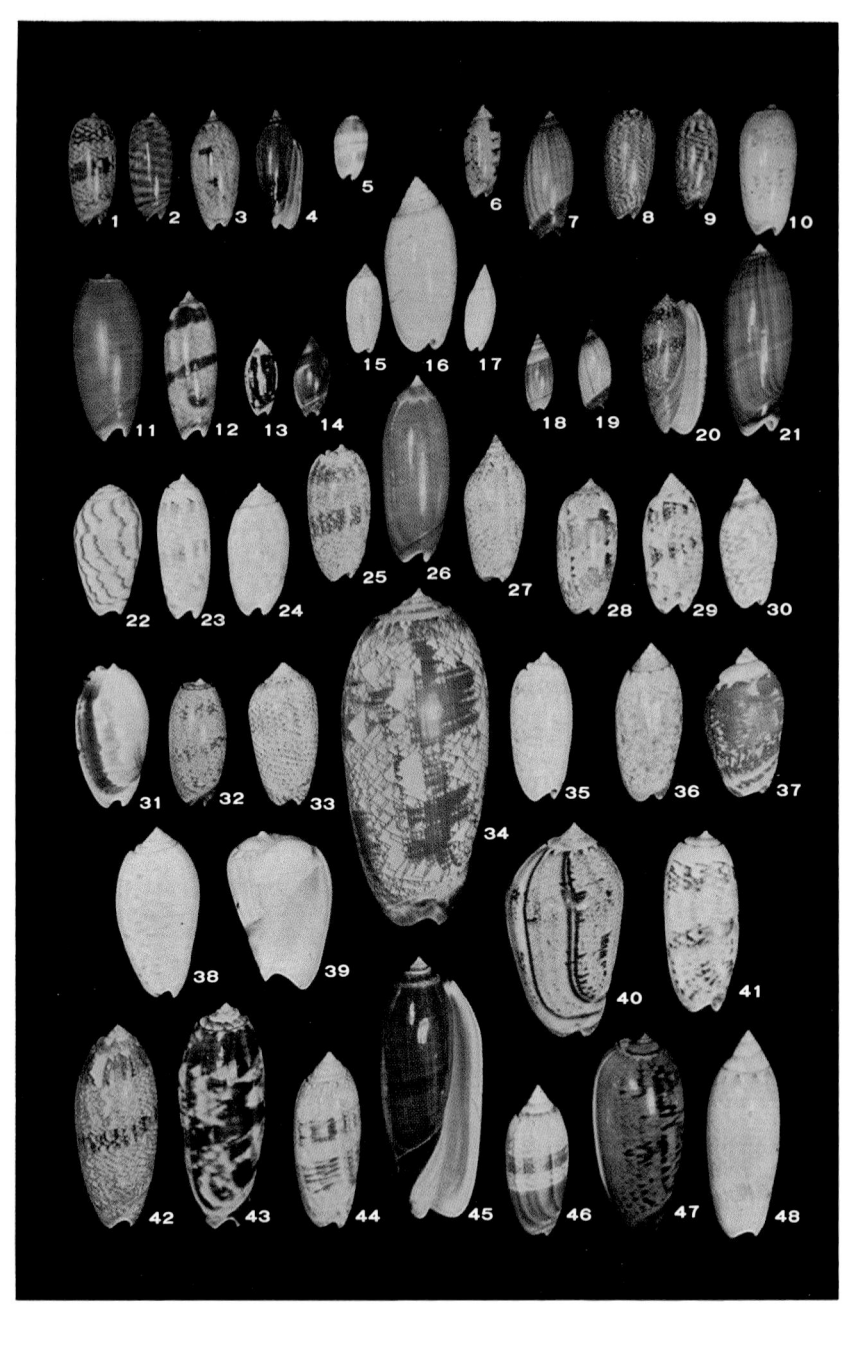

PLATE 12

Plate 12 (cont.)

32. *Oliva oliva* L. P.I. Syns: *O. maura* Lam. and *O. cincta* Dautz. Olive to black and variably mottled. Oblong and ovate. Spire expressed, with raised callus near lip. See also No. 11.   2″ .50

33. *Oliva venulata* Lam. Panamic Prov. Terminology unsettled. Perhaps a variety of *O. spicata* with low spire. Brownish dots.
2″ .50

34. *Oliva porphyria* L. Panamic Prov. The largest, and also the type species of the genus. Unmistakable as the Camp Olive. Pink tints on brown. Much prized. Not common.   3½″ 4.00

35. *Oliva tricolor* Lam. Indo-Pac. Orange and bluish mottling on white.   2″ .75

36. *Oliva annulata* Gmel. P.I. Syn: *O. emicator intricata* Dautz. Brown mottling on cream. Salmon-colored ends and interior.   1½″ .50

37. *Olivancillaria gibbosa* Born. Ceylon. Brown. White callus on spire and columella.
2″ .75

38. *Oliva tigrina* Lam. E.Afr. Ovate. Mottling of blue-grey on white.
1¾″ .50

39. *Olivancillaria brasiliana* Lam. Brazil. Streaked fawn. Triangular, thick, and callused.   1½″ 1.00

40. *Oliva incrassata* Sol. Panamic Prov.

Syn: *O. angulata* Lam. Dark marks and mottling. Thick. Angular shoulder.
2½″ 1.00

41. *Oliva sayana* Ravenel. Fla. Syn: *O. litterata* Lam. Yellowish to white. Two brown bands of V's. Cylindrical. See also No. 44.   2″ .35

42. *Oliva textilina* Lam. P.I. Cream. Fine, intercrossed lines. Two bands. 2½″ .60

43. *Oliva erythrostoma saturata* Dautz. Indo-Pac. Variety with darker lines and patches.   3″ .75

44. *Oliva sayana* Ravenel. Fla. Syn: *O. litterata* Lam. Brown bands and network of grey, rarely yellow. Popular names are Lettered Olive, Panama Roll, and Golden Olive for the yellow ones. See also No. 41.
2″ .35, yellow 5.00 and up

45. *Oliva erythrostoma marrati* Johnson. P.I. "Black" form. Any olive which covers itself with a black nacre is called popularly a Black Olive. See also No. 21. 3″ 2.50

46. *Oliva reticularis greenwayae* Clench. Cuba. Brown middle and lower bands. Axial zig-zags on white.   2″ .75

47. *Oliva irisans* Lam. P.I. Grey, sharply zig-zagging axial lines. White inside.
2½″ 1.00

48. *Olivancillaria acuminata* Lam. W.Afr. Slim. Nebulous grey zig-zags. Brownish end band.   1½″ 1.00

Plate 13

1. *Voluta (Amoria) elliotti* Sow. W.Aust. One of the rare and well-marked members of the large group of *Volutidae* which come only from Australian waters. Unbroken flowing chestnut lines from top of the shoulder to the tip, all against a yellowish background.   3″   Price variable 10.00

2. *Voluta (Volutoconus) grossi* Ired. Queensland, Aust. The color and form are notable. A slim, smooth, glossy shell with a few indistinct white tents seeming to underly three interrupted bands of orange-red and a network of red. Interior is whitish. Columella with about three plaits. An unusual feature is a bluish band on the under side near the top of the spire with its needle-sharp point. Rare.   4″   35.00 and up

3. *Voluta (Amoria) grayi* Ludbrook. W. Aust. Syns: *V. volva* Chem. and *V. pallida* Gray. The name given by Gray well describes this slim translucent greyish shell. The pale orange of the interior of the lip may show through. Further inside the interior is coffee brown. Faint striations may show in the spire and on the body whorl.   3″   8.00

4. *Voluta (Ericusa) fulgetrum* Sow., 1825. Aust. Glistening cream-colored with brown zig-zag marks. Four post-nuclear whorls, the smallest beginning almost at a point and widening as the whorls descend. Columella with three delicate plaits. Interior is salmon color. The embryo of this shell is especially interesting. Rare.
  5″   Price variable 15.00 and up

5. *Voluta (Aulicina) vespertilio* L. P.I. Bat Volute. A color series of this shell is most attractive. Color ranges through dark greenish brown to orange-yellow, the color of the specimen photographed here. Commonest of the *Volutidae*, yet this is a beautiful shell. 3″ occasionally larger   Plain .25, Pronged .75, Rare colors much higher in price.

6. *Voluta (Harpulina) arausaica* Sol. Ceylon. Syn: *Voluta vexillum* Gmel. Unique in its marking of orange rings on white. The spire is conical with small pointed apex. Shoulder and spire with somewhat sup-

pressed nodules. Columella with six or more smaller to larger plaits. Rare.
  3″   8.00 and up

7. *Voluta (Aulicina) nivosa* Lam. N.W. Aust. Syn: *V. nivosa oblita* E. H. Smith. This shell has long been called *Voluta norrisi* Sow, and the name is still widely used. Buff color, with greyish brown patches that form distinct bands. Interior dark brown, shading inward to grey-brown. Columella is peach color, with four plaits. Spire is edged with sharp nodules. Not common. 2½″—3″.   3″   5.00

8. *Voluta (Voluta) musica* L. Trinidad to Venezuela. Buff or yellow under brownish pattern. Across the stocky shell run sets of about five lines resembling the musical staff. Squarish black dots look like medieval notes. Strong, smooth, light-colored nodules circle the shoulder and spire. Black squares on the yellowish lip. Yellow columella with many plaits. Shells from different localities show wide variation in form and coloring. Scarce.   2¼″   5.00, 3¾″   20.00

9. *Voluta (Cymbiolacca) pulchra* Sow. Aust. Syn: *V. pulchra woolacottae* Mc Michael. This choice shell has the distinguished charm of a pink dimity dress. The body color is pink, tented with white. Three faint bands of dull rose color are sparsely dotted with accents which are almost black. The raised spire is crowned at the edge with nine sharp horns which are molded down gracefully into the body. Not common.   2″   3.00, 2¾″   5.00

10. *Voluta (Alcithoe) swainsoni* Marwick. New Zealand. Cream-colored, with scribbled brown markings falling into three bands. Smooth rounded shoulders and wrinkled spire. Lip is thickened and turned over. Columella has about five plaits and is turned back in a fold over the canal.
  5½″   4.50

11. *Voluta (Aulica) aulica* Sow. Sulu Sea. One of the most distinguished and most wanted of all the *Volutidae*. This shell is valued for its large size, its opulent shape, its glisten, and its rich color variations which range through many shades of cream, pink,

Plate 13 (cont.)

orange, and rich red. Generally there is some mottling in cloud forms arranged in two bands, but occasionally specimens that are entirely red are found. Even the less perfect specimens of this shell are highly valued, perfect specimens being exceedingly rare. No. 12 is a white variety of *V. aulica* Sow. Grade A specimens 3″ 18.00, 4″ 28.00, 5″ 50.00 and up. Entirely-red specimens are higher priced. Good Grade B specimens 25% less, and good Grade C specimens 50% less.

12. Same as No. 11

13. *Voluta (Cymbiolacca) wisemani* Brazier. N.E.Aust. The refinement of this shell in form and coloring is amazing. The two weak bands of faint orange markings on white and the translucence of the inner lip give the effect of fine porcelain. The body whorl is slim, rather than plump like *Voluta aulica*, and the horns, or shoulder, and spire are sharp. The milk white columella has four plaits. Rare. 2½″ 16.00

14. *Voluta (Aulicina) sophiae* Gray. N.W. Aust. A shiny surface of light grey-brown, with two bands of darker brown characteristically edged with lines of distant, almost square, black dots. A slightly bluish cast to the almost white mottling of the whole shell gives it a scarcely perceptible blue-grey cast. Sharp horns on crown and spire. Interior of lip edged with brown, merging into whitish. Columella with four plaits.
2¼″ 5.00 and up

15. *Voluta (Volutocorona) imperialis* Lightfoot. P.I. Large specimens seldom have the perfection of the small 3″ ones shown here. Typical marking is of wavy chocolate-colored lines and patches forming bands. The rounded top of the spire looks like a chocolate drop. The horns are sharp and turned inward. Large specimens are seldom seen without slightly broken horns, which are not too noticeable in large shells.
Up to 8″ About 1.25 an inch

16. *Voluta (Alcithoe) depressa* Suter. N. New Zealand. Light brown, with dark brown markings in waves and patches forming an upper and lower band. Shoulder and spire have strong nodules. The edge of the thickened lip is patched with brown. The columella has four plaits merging into the inner lip which forms a fold back over the canal. Rare. 3″ 6.00 and up

17. *Voluta (Amoria) maculata* Swainson. Queensland, Aust. Syn: *V. caroli* Ired. Smooth, shiny, and yellowish. Circled with bands of long spots. Aperture is straight and lengthened. Interior is yellow to brown. Columella has four plaits. Rare.
2½″ 6.00

18. *Voluta (Adelomelon) ancilla* Sol. Uruguay. A unique shell from cold waters of Southern South America. Unlike the sleek *Volutidae* of Australia, this one is prone to showing growth lines and a worn finish. Nevertheless, its tall whitish spire and shining yellow body whorl, decorated with rippling brown lines, are of distinguished form. The interior of the thin lip is peach color, as is the three-plaited columella. The best specimens are especially rare. 4″—7½″.
6″ 8.00

19. *Voluta (Amoria) undulata* Lam. S.Aust. The ground is cream to golden and has thin dark lines forming graceful parallel undulations of intriguing pattern. Interior is peach color. 3″ 3.00

20. *Voluta (Aulicina) rutila* Brod. N.E. Aust. A stunning shell with whitish background completely suffused with red veinings and banded with indeterminate patches of rich red. The shell is smooth and shining, even over the shoulders which are without horns or nodules. The interior is salmon color. 3″ 8.00

PLATE 13

Plate 14

1. *Voluta (Adelomelon) becki* Brod. Brazil. Brown, with peach on columella and inside. Dull striated exterior. Lip is thin and fragile. This specimen is 8½". Rare.
8½" 9.00, 12" and over 15.00 and up

2. *Voluta (Voluta) ebraea* L. Brazil. Hebrew Volute. Thick and stocky, with bands of randomly painted striations of dark brown thought to resemble Hebrew characters. Five or more heavy plaits on columella. Interior is cream to flesh. Rare.
4½" 9.00

3. *Voluta (Pachycymbiola) braziliana* Lam. Brazil. Heavy and thick. Body is dull, with rough growth lines. Smooth columella. Peach color interior. Interesting 2" translucent egg sacs which are sometimes preserved in formaldehyde. 4" 3.50

4. *Voluta (Mesericusa) sowerbyi* Kiener. S. Aust. Syn: *V. fusiformis* Swain. Slim and pinkish, with lengthwise chestnut zig-zags. Spire has six whorls. 4" 3.50, 7" 7.00

5. *Voluta (Fulgoraria) cancellata* Kuroda & Habe. Japan. Fusiform. Light brownish with neat descending pleatings and fine circling lines. 3" 2.00

6. *Voluta (Cymbium) glans* Gmel. W.Afr. Syn: *V. (Cymbium) proboscidalis* Lam. Handsome flaring peach aperture. Concave spiral crown. A "varnish" finish is laid over scratches and particles. Scarce where caught. Large specimens seldom reach other countries. 5" 5.00, 11" 16.00

7. *Voluta (Volutocorona) nobilis* Sol. Singapore. Syn: *V. scapha* Gmel., but not *V. scafa* Sol. which is *Cymbium cymbium* L. Dark flesh color, with thin descending brown lines of wavy zig-zags. Heavy white callus on parietal wall. Four plaits. Some shells are almost conical, and others have a flaring wing. Rare. 3½" 6.50

8. *Voluta (Volutocorona) imperialis* Lightfoot. P.I. Syn: *V. imperialis robinsona* Burch. Variety *robinsona* has waving zigzagging axial lines against warm pink. Described in "Minutes of Conchological Club of Southern California #140."
Up to 8" About 1.60 an inch

9. *Voluta (Ericusa) papillosa* Swain. S. Aust. Lacelike pattern on dorsum, rather than the dark squarish marking of *V. fulgetrum*. Columella has three to five plaits. 5½" 12.50

10. *Voluta (Cymbiolista) hunteri* Ired. N.S.W., Aust. Syn: *V. marmorata* Swainson. Handsome, glossy, and pinkish-orange. Bands of chestnut markings. Nodules on shoulder and spire. Wide oblong aperture. 4"—6½". 5" 4.00 and up

11. *Voluta (Zidonia) dufresnei* Donovan. Uruguay. Syn: *V. angulata* Swain. One of the most distinctive of the *Volutidae* in both form and color. Body whorl is flesh color, with streaking or "mountains" of pale blue-grey. Wide rounded shoulders. Spire, columella, and lip are orange. A pointed spiral callus is produced beyond the tip, but is often broken off. All-over enameling of shiny nacre. 6" 6.00

12. *Voluta (Cymbium) cisium* Menke. W. Afr. Syn: *V. (Cymbium) gracilis* Brod. Grey, with dark brown clouding, concave spire, and button nucleus. Callus on rounded columellar wall. Flaring wing-shaped lip. Rare. 5" 12.00

13. *Voluta (Fulgoraria) concinna* Brod. Japan. Slim. Light brown, with darker bands of axial striae. Sloping shoulders. Spire has rounded axial ribs. 5½" 3.75

14. *Voluta (Cymbium) pepo* Sol. W.Afr. Syn: *V. (Cymbium) neptuni* Gmel. White callus on parietal wall. Shiny, with peach color within aperture and on columella. Lip extends beyond nuclear end in unique pink cup to a faint nucleus. Rare. 7" 15.00

15. *Voluta (Fulgoraria) mentiens* Fulton. Japan. Flesh color, with upper, middle, and lower bands of few brown markings. Upper half with rounded ribs. Opening more than half length of shell. 4" 2.50

16. *Voluta (Cymbium) cymbium* L. W.Afr. Syn: *V. (Cymbium) porcina* Lam. Very unusual form. Grey-brown, with light brown callus. Shiny brown columella and interior. Unique wing-shaped aperture and thin-edged spiral crown. Scarce. 5¼" 10.00

PLATE 14

Plate 15

1. *Xancus pyrum* L. Ceylon & India. Syn: *Turbinella pyrum* L. One of the few shells about which there is a whole book: *The Sacred Chank of India* by James Hornell, Madras Fisheries Bulletin 7, 1914 (out of print). The shell is pear-shaped, heavy, white, sometimes with a few brownish dots.
3⅛″ 4.00, 5½″ 8.00

2. *Xancus angulatus* Sol. Bahamas to Fla. & Yucatan, E. Mex. West Indies Chank. Syn: *Turbinella scolyma* Gmel. Most superb in sculpture of almost all large shells. Resembles the *Volutidae.* Attractive deep cream to pale yellow, with pinkish aperture. Heavy. Strong plaits on columella. A magnificent shell of 7″ to 14″. 8″ 6.00

3. *Voluta (Alcithoe) arabica* Gmel. N. Zealand. Syn: *V. pacifica* Perry. Apex is pointed. Nine strong nodules on body whorl. Brownish splashes. 4″ 4.00

4. *Voluta (Fulgoraria) daviesi* Fulton. Japan. Slender, with vertical striae. Banded by squarish patches. 5″ 3.25

5. *Voluta (Livonia) mammilla* Sow. E. Aust. Syn: *V. mamilla* Gray. Thin, wide aperture and large apical knob. Brown markings on light buff. 8½″ 9.00

6. *Voluta (Cymbiolena) magnifica* Gebauer. E.Aust. Found in deep water. Has a wide aperture and a pointed apex. Cream to pinkish. About four bands of brown wavy markings. 7″ 8.00

7. *Voluta (Melo) aethiopica* L. Indo-Pac. Syn: *V. (Melo) broderipi* Gray. Swollen, with wide aperture. At apex, short pointed spines bunch together over the low spire. Yellow-brown, with chestnut bands.
7½″ 4.50

8. *Voluta (Livonia) mammilla* Sow. E. Aust. Syn: *V. mamilla leucostoma* Maybloom. Scarce color form.
8″—12″ 30.00 and up

9. *Voluta (Melo) amphora* Sol. N.E.Aust. Syns: *V. (Melo) diadema* Lam. and *V. (Melo) flammea* Röd. "Bailer shell" used by natives to bail boats and to carry water. Eight or more hollow spines on periphery of last whorl. Spines are discontinued and replaced by ridge on body whorl near tip. Ivory, marked with light to dark brown.
5″—10″ 3.00—8.00

10. Same as No. 9.

Plate 16

1. *Mitra ferruginea* Lam. Japan. White, with orange bands and patches. Circled with heavy ridges. A stocky shell with thickened nodules on lip. The ridges on the columella continue to form plaits.
1½″ 1.00

2. *Mitra cardinalis* Gmel. P.I. Cardinal's Miter. White, circled with many rows of square reddish-to-chestnut marks. Five plaits on columella. Sharp pointed teeth on edge of the lip. Inside is white.
1¾″ 1.00

3. *Mitra (Pterygia) dactylis* L. P.I. Brownish, circled with fine dark lines. Smooth

over shoulder and over low spire. Lip is thickened. White interior. Six plaits.
1¼″ .75

4. *Mitra adusta* Lam. P.I. Smooth. Shaped like a bud about to open, with edges of crown closely serrated. A neatly formed Miter. Peach-colored inside and out. Dark lines about the whorls with chestnut streaks cutting across them. 1¼″ .50

5. *Mitra (Chrysame) ambigua* Swainson. Japan. Yellowish, with white bands and five lines, or ridges, across the whorls. Plaited columella. Teeth along the lip.
1¾″ .75

PLATE 15

Plate 16 (cont.)

6. *Mitra mitra* L. Indo-Pac. Syn: *M. episcopalis* L. Lavishly decorated over its whole sleek smooth surface with squares and patches of bright red against pure white. Small orifice. Peach interior. Columella with about four plaits. A series of Miters have been named for church dignitaries because of a fancied resemblance to their ritual headgear. 1¾"—6".
2½" .35, 5" 2.00

7. *Mitra nucea* Gmel. Indo-Pac. Nut Miter. Flesh color shell with brown bands. Smooth body merges into smooth spire. Tiny, dark-tipped serrations on the lip. 1¼" 1.25

8. *Mitra belcheri* Hinds. W.Mex. This magnificent shell is most popular of the Miters of the Panamic shell province. If two specimens were shown side by side, they could show the bared flesh-colored shell itself and the shell clothed with the contrasting black periostracum. Both would show the circling channeled lines cut in over the whole shell as, whorl by whorl, it mounts gracefully to its high spire. This shell deserves a better fate than to be named after a Captain Belcher and might more appropriately have been given such an Aztec title as Mitra netzalhualcoyotli! To 5". 4½" 4.00

9. *Mitra lamarcki* Deshayes. Mozambique. White inside and out, and circled by faint ridges ending in fine teeth on the lip. Whorls of typical Miter form get gradually smaller in the spire. Indeterminately banded with white and with interrupted light and dark brown. 1⅝" 1.00

10. *Mitra papalis* L. Indo-Pac. Pope's Miter. Superb appearance, with dark red, squarish markings that run together into lengthened patches, all against white. Mitral coronet of distinct white points. About five plaits. Peach interior.
3½" 2.00

11. *Mitra zaca* Broderip. W.Mex. Peace Miter (*zaca* is an Indian word for "peace"). One of the largest Panamic Miters, this is a smooth shell with smooth shoulders lacking the lines of its companion piece, *Mitra belcheri*. Fine contrast is obtained in a pair, one with and one without the black periostracum. Peach-colored whorls darken gradually to the spire. To 5". 3¼" 2.75

12. *Mitra ornata coccineum* Reeve. Okinawa. This shell varies throughout in color from orange-yellow, to yellow and a bit of white. Lines cross the body, and the tall spire appears crumpled into ridges.
2" 4.00

13. *Mitra plicaria* L. P.I. Striking pattern of circling rows of black hyphens with a central, or intermediate, broad band of dark brown against the white shell. The pattern varies from much white to much brown. Black markings show through against the orange lip inside. 1½" .75

14. *Mitra stictica* Link. Indo-Pac. Syn: *M. pontificalis* Lam. Pontifical Miter. Bands of squarish orange patches circle a cream ground. About four plaits. Sharp serration on edge of lip. Interior is peach color. The spire, a series of crowns edged with nodules, slopes slightly inward.
2" 1.25

15. *Mitra tessellata* Mart. P.I. Tiled Miter. All-over orange-brown with descending wavy streaks of rich brown on a slightly glistening surface. Lip is serrated. About five plaits. Interior is peach color. To 4".
3" 3.00

PLATE 16

Plate 17

1. *Conus stercusmuscarum* L. Indo-Pac. Fly-Specked Cone. Smooth rounded cone with a beige to white background, spotted with black dots, sometimes in distinct circling lines and sometimes so close as to form dark waves or patches. Strong orange deep in aperture. The crown, if felt with the finger, is smooth and without the nodules of *Conus arenatus* Hwass, which is stockier and has smaller dots.
2″ 1.25

2. *Conus namocanus* Hwass. E.Afr. Syn: *C. laevigatus* Sow. Smooth Cone. Wide at shoulders. Low spire. Glabrous, with light yellowish upper band and irregular patches of olive brown, with same color in wide band at the tip.
2″ 1.25

3. *Conus planorbis* Born. P.I. Brownish yellow, with bands of lighter color. Dark markings on top, pale base, and lavender inside.
2″ .85

4. *Conus gubernator* Hwass. E.Afr. Syn: *C. terminus* Lam. Very variable marking. See also Plate 18, No. 6.
2¼″ 1.50

5. *Conus pennaceus* Born. Indo-Pac. Syns: *C. omaria* Hwass. and *C. magnificus* Reeve. Slender brown cone, lavishly marked with small white tenting clustered to approximate bands up and down and about the body.
1¾″ 1.25

6. *Conus regius* Gmel. Fla. Syn: *C. nebulosus* Hwass. The bandings of bluish white on a chestnut brown intermingle in a fascinating array of color. A thick cone with wide shoulders but a thin lip.
1¾″ 2.00

7. *Conus zeylanicus* Gmel. E.Afr. Obese Cone. Syn: *C. obesus* Hwass. Thick, plump, and broad shouldered. White, with two bands of intricate waving lavender. Net work darkened with black marking.
2¼″ 3.00

8. *Conus marmoreus nocturnus* Solander. Philippines. A tented cone with wide bandings of dark and white. Since this is very desirable as a cabinet specimen, collectors may ignore identification controversy and give it whatever temporary label they prefer.

The specimen shown corresponds to the color picture and description under this name in Reeve's monumental *Conchologica Iconica.*
2″ 2.00

9. *Conus ammiralis* L. Sulu Archipelago. Tented Admiral Cone. Something of a jewel-set effect is given by the mosaic of large and small white tents showing against broad bands of rich brown and narrow bands of light brown. A collectors' favorite which, in earlier days, brought fabulous prices. Uncommon. Large and fine specimens rare.
2″ 4.50, 2½″ 7.00

10. *Conus augur* Sol. E.Afr. Augury Cone. Syn: *C. auger* Hwass. Stocky ivory-colored cone. All the bands are circled with close lines of fine dots. Two black bands seldom complete and uninterrupted and usually of large hieroglyphical forms might do as well as anything else for the purposes of augury. Not common.
2″ 5.00

11. *Conus sozoni* Bartsch. Gulf of Mex. Yellow-brown marking and bandings. Sloped spire. See also Plate 21, No. 1. Rare.
2″ 10.00

12. *Conus recurvus* Brod. W.Mex. Recurved Cone. White, with bands of fantastic brown patches. Distinctive shape suggests its name since sides of the body whorl are slightly concave. Spire is moderately high with concave slope, each whorl being channeled. Line from shoulder to tip of the lip curves outward.
2½″ 3.50

13. *Conus generalis* L. Indo-Pac. General (Standard or Ordinary) Cone. A highly variable shell. Often very attractive, as in the specimen shown which has wide orange bands and narrower bands of white variably marked with black. A slim cone, usually with a high, pointed spire.
2½″ 1.75

14. *Conus maldivus* Hwass. E.Afr. & Maldive Islands. Maldive Cone. This cone is excessively variable. It is best recognized by its general, rather than its particular appearance. Most of the obvious characteristics of the usual variations of *C. generalis* appear, but in a less clear-cut form. The brown bands are less regular,

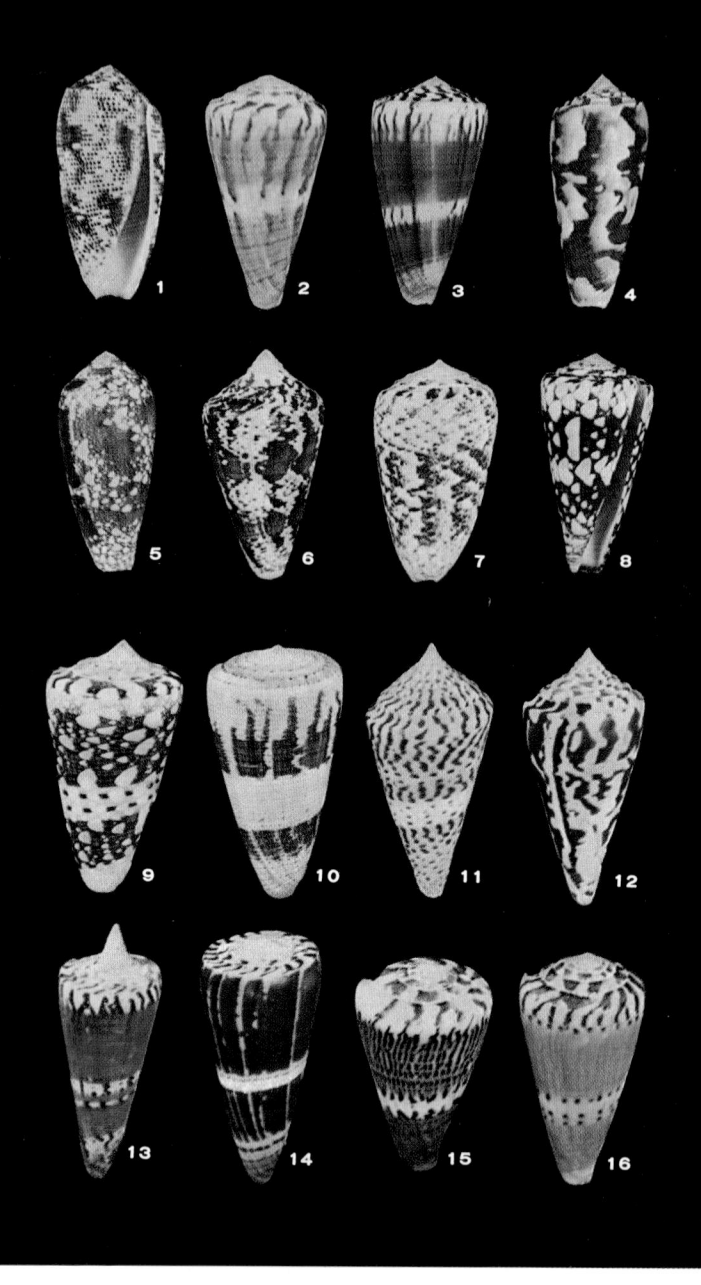

PLATE 17

Plate 17 (cont.)

and the white bands may or may not appear at the tip, middle, and shoulder. Streaking of brown or white may descend from top to tip. Crown is usually flatter, and spire lower and less pointed.   2″—3″   1.50—2.50

15. *Conus capitaneus* L. Indo-Pac. Captain Cone. Syn: *C. chemnitzii* Dillwyn. Broad at shoulders. Attractive but variable coloration. Background is brown, varying to shades of yellowish and faint green. Fine dark striations often descend the body whorl. One white band near the middle, another at the shoulder, both with dark

brown hieroglyphic markings at the edges, not the dots of *Conus mustellinus* Hwass. Often dark or purplish at the top and on the interior.   2″   1.00

16. *Conus mustellinus* Hwass. Indo-Pac. Weasel Cone. Mustard color, perhaps with a faint tinge of green. Narrow shoulder. Whitish body bands with circles of black dots. Differs from *Conus capitaneus* L. in background color and by the three bands of dots, one of which may be vestigial, that edge the white band of the body whorl. Smooth spire, checkered with black and white. Interior is white.   1½″   1.00

Plate 18

1. *Conus thalassiarchus* Sow. Indo-Pac. Untented Admiral Cone. Alternate bands of yellow and of white scribbled with fine yellow dots and lines. Shoulder and crown are mottled with dark brown. Tip is brown to purple. Interior is light yellow.
    3″   3.50

2. *Conus episcopus* Hwass. P.I. Slim, dark brown, white-tented cone. Shoulders and spire are rounded. See also Plate 20, No. 2.
    2½″   2.50

3. *Conus quercinus* Sol. Indo-Pac. Yellow surface covered with minute circular lines. Slightly elevated apex.   2¼″   1.00

4. *Conus terebra* Born. Indo-Pac. Terebra Cone. Syn: *C. terebellum* Mart. Slim, dull white cone with gently curving spire. Circled with faint wide yellow bands and incised lines. Purple tip.   2½″   2.50

5. *Conus virgatus* Reeve. S.Calif. to Ecuador. White, shaded with light tinting of orange. Brown wavy axial stripes, sometimes vestigial or absent. Fine circling lines help produce the silken effect seen by moving the shell in the light.   2″   1.50

6. *Conus gubernator* Hwass. E.Afr. Governor Cone. Large, slim cone with smooth rounding shoulders sloping into a pointed spire. Very variable with the brown sometimes dark, sometimes light, and the white

occasionally tinged with blue. At its best, a very handsome cone decorated as if a darkened sky with summer clouds. *Conus gubernator* Brug. lacks the definite circling lines that are seen on *Conus striatus* L. See also Plate 17, No. 4.   2¼″   1.50

7. *Conus distans* Hwass. Indo-Pac. Slightly attenuated in the middle. Reddish, yellow, or ash color. Base is stained blackish violet. Spire is coronated. Apex is flatly truncated.
    2½″   1.00, 3″   2.00

8. *Conus marmoreus bandanus* Hwass. Indo-Pac. A tented cone, with some tents farther apart showing more black in two bands.   2½″   1.00, 4″   2.00

9. *Conus orbignyi* Audouin. Japan. D'Orbigny's Cone. Dull-surfaced cone with a high, neatly coronated, sharp spire which adds to the length of this slim shell. White, circled with corrugations and with brown bands and lines of squarish dots.
    2″   .75

10. *Conus australis* Holten. Japan. Slim glossy white cone, circled with lightly cut ridges. Banded with alternate circles of wide and narrow, irregular brown mottling.
    3″   2.00

11. *Conus striatus* L. Indo-Pac. Deep, prominent striae all over. Whitish, stained with rose and streaked and mottled with black.

PLATE 18

Plate 18 (cont.)

Spire is deeply canaliculated. 2½″ 1.00

12. *Conus miles* L. Indo-Pac. Soldier Cone. Much admired, this broad-shouldered cone is white, with bands of light and dark brown and waved filaments of brown from top to tip. 2″ 1.00

13. *Conus geographus* L. Indo-Pac. Probably the most virulent of the poisonous cones. Thin texture. Swollen. Spire is coronated. Often flesh color, blotched, and reticulated with reddish brown. Apex is rose. 3″—5½″. 3″ 1.50

Plate 19

1. *Conus betulinus* L. Indo-Pac. Birch Bark Cone. One of the few *Conidae* that grow large, heavy, and broad at the shoulders. Orange bands, interbanded with light yellow ones which are interrupted with dark, squarish or irregular dots. Thin lip. White interior. The color is usually finest in the smaller specimens. 2¼″—6″.
2¼″ 1.25, 5″ 3.50

2. *Conus litteratus* L. Indo-Pac. Lettered Cone. White, with bands of squarish dots, usually in even lines. The most attractive specimens are some which have a banding of peach color. The tip is purple, stained, and pointed (not truncated), which characteristics distinguish it from *Conus leopardus*. 3″ 1.00

3. *Conus marmoreus* L. Indo-Pac. Marble Cone. Milk white triangles on night black. Not only do practically all collectors own one, but others use it to set off flowers or to add an ornament in home decoration. The pattern is unique and has no rival.
2½″ 1.00

4. *Conus leopardus* Röd. Indo-Pac. Leopard Cone. Syn: *C. millepunctatus* Lam. Large, stocky white cone with well-lined bands of black markings. Some of these are even lines of dots, some squarish, and some hieroglyphical. The tip is unstained white and is cut off, or truncated, which characteristics distinguish it from *Conus litteratus* L. 3″—9″. 3½″ 1.25

5. *Conus aulicus* L. Indo-Pac. Courtly Cone. One of the largest of the *Conidae*, this is reddish brown with white tent-shaped markings. It may be distinguished from *C. episcopus* by noticing that in *Conus aulicus* the greatest circumference is near

mid-point, whereas in *C. episcopus* it is higher up near the shoulders. Rare. To 6″.
4½″ 10.00

6. *Conus vexillum* Gmel. Indo-Pac. Flag Cone. Syn: *C. canonicus* Röd. One of the larger *Conidae*. Stocky, with broad shoulders. Predominantly streaky orange-brown, with two bands of irregular white patches, one at the shoulders. White and brown patterned spire. Occasionally to 5½″, usually 1¾″—4¾″. 2½″ 1.50

7. *Conus imperialis* L. Indo-Pac. Imperial Cone. White, with many bandings of dark lines, of dark dots, and of dark dashes superimposed on the white ground and on the wide bands of light brown. Not a shiny cone. Stocky. Crowned with points. Growth lines usually visible. A faint bluish tinge in some shells, especially near the brown tip. 2″—3¾″. 2¾″ 2.00

8. *Conus textile* L. Indo-Pac. Cloth-of-Gold Cone. Syn: *C. archiepiscopus* Hwass. Leader of the tented cones. The golden ground of this shell is lined with irregular dark descending lines at right angles to the tents outlined in a network of thin brown lines. The over-all pattern gives an appearance of faint banding. Fatalities from the bite of this "poison cone" have been reported. 1¼″—4″. 2″ 1.00

9. *Conus textile verriculum* Reeve. Indo-Pac. A variety of *C. textile* L. with large tenting of white. 1¼″—4″. 2″ 1.50

10. *Conus nicobaricus* Hwass. Indo-Pac. Nicobar Island Cone. Pinkish white, with all-over tentings and network of fine lines. Banded with two or three interrupted black bands of varying intensity. Yellowish with-

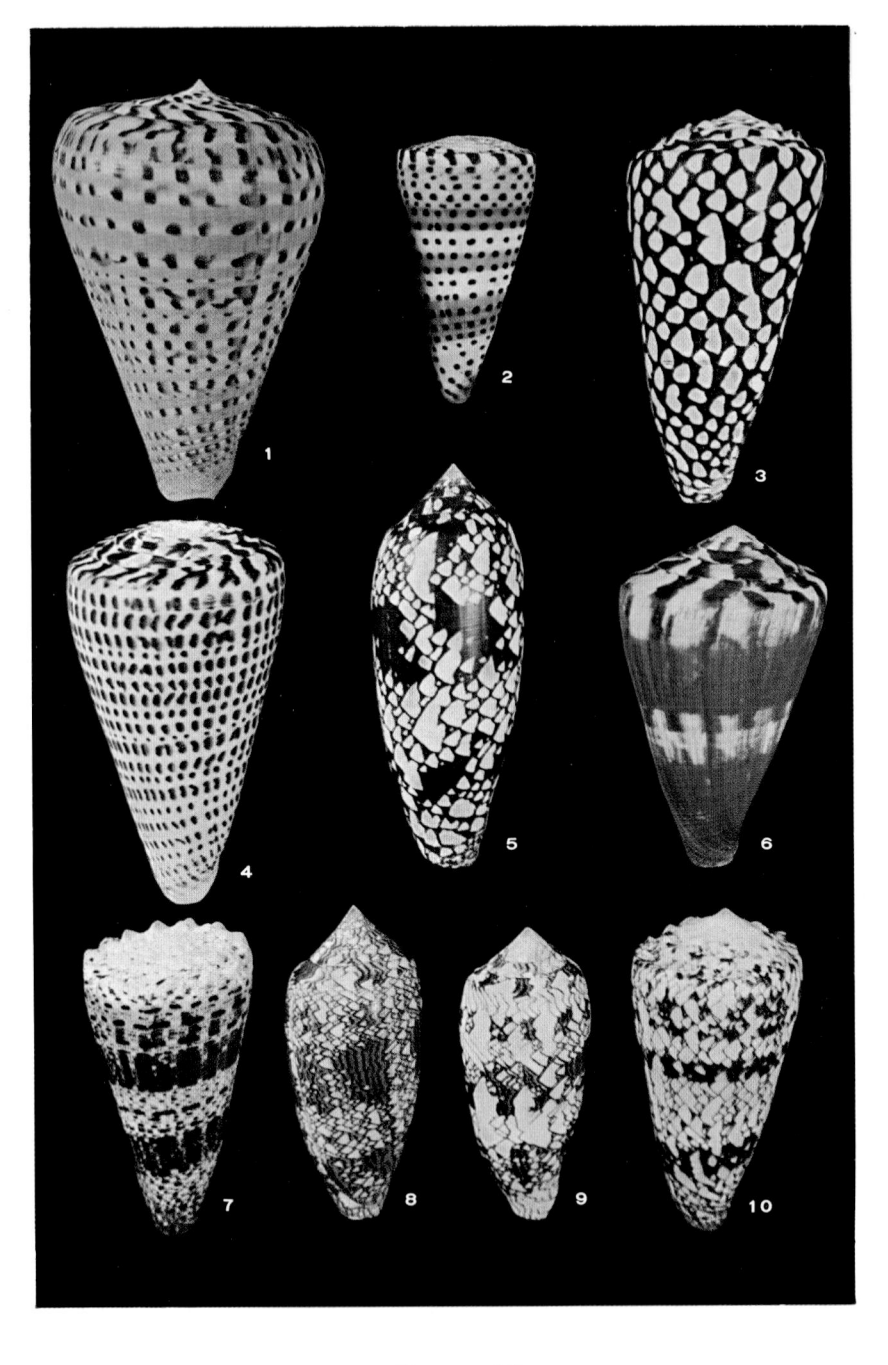

PLATE 19

Plate 19 (cont.)

in. In his *Conchologica Iconica*, Reeve describes this shell thus: "Shell turbinated, whitish, irregularly reticulated with dusky black, doubly banded; spire flat, depressed, apex somewhat raised, whorls concavely canaliculated around the upper part, interior tinged with yellow." Amateurs are fond of setting up their own standards by which they equate this cone with or differentiate it from *Conus araneosus* Sol. Not common.　　　　　　　　　　　2″　3.00

Plate 20

1. *Conus purpurascens* Sow. W. Mex. Chiefly bluish purple inside, but tinges pervade exterior in irregular bands going up, down, and around. Irregular brown patches suffuse the paler ground color.
1¾″ 1.00

2. *Conus episcopus* Hwass. P.I. White tents run in waving patches, down against a rich chestnut background and up into a sloping spire. See also Plate 18, No. 2.
2½″ 2.50

3. *Conus spectrum* L. Syn: *C. broderipii* Reeve. Rich brown markings all over on white. Heavier brown patches in two bands. Roundly molded cone. Flat spire with a sharp point. Wide aperture with thin lip.
2″ 1.75

4. *Conus praelatus* Hwass. E.Afr. Prelate's Cone. Brown patches wander among vertical and transverse bands. Tented with white run in with blue, a rare color in cones. One of the most distinctive and lovely of all cones. Scarce.
2″ 1.75

5. *Conus ione* Fulton. Japan. Suffused with pale violet, and so unique. Mottled with two brown bands. Named from *ion*, Greek for "violet."
2″ Fine color 2.00

6. *Conus spectrum pica* A. Adams & Reeve. P.I. Same shape as *C. spectrum* L. but white with black markings down the cone in a wavy zig-zag.
1⅜″ 2.75

7. *Conus magus* L. Syns: *C. raphanus* Hwass. and *C. tenellus* Chem. *C. magus* wanders into many varieties which have been assiduously named on slim justification. It goes into creams, yellows, and browns and affects bands and mottlings and various forms bewildering in identification.
2″ .75

8. *Conus ximenes* Gray. Panamic Prov. Syn: *C. interruptus* Brod. & Sow. Flesh-colored, circled with brown dots and dashes. Purple interior. Well-elevated spire with sharp point.
1½″ .75

9. *Conus lautus* Reeve. S.Afr. Flesh color, darkened with bands of orange which are circled with interrupted chestnut lines and marked with brown elongated triangles on some bands. Specimens are usually beach. High smooth spire. Here classified, according to Turton, as a member of the *rosaceus* complex.
1½″ 1.25

10. *Conus ebraeus* L. P.I. Syn: *C. quadratus* Perry. Small, but of striking appearance due to bands of interrupted black on flesh-colored body and spire. Marks resemble Hebrew characters.
1¼″ .50

11. *Conus varius* L. P.I. A shiny shell which looks rough because of circles of nodules and dark dots. There is a crown of nodules circling a high spire. Two blackish bands, the upper one looking like dark clouds, decorate a very pale brownish surface. Rare.
1¼″ 2.00

12. *Conus coronatus* Gmel. Indo-Pac. Syn: *C. minimus* Born. Variable. Light blue-grey to beige. Dark olive to brown mottling. Nodules circle shoulder and spire.
1″ .50

13. *Conus nobilis* L. Indo-Pac. Syn: *C. cordigera* Sow. Almost a century ago Reeve ticked off this one, saying "Variety A" is more or less inclining to yellow, profusely painted with white, triangularly rounded, and scattered with spots. "Variety B" is pale lemon color, with spots large and heart-shaped, and with tranverse lines almost obsolete. Rare.
1¼″ 5.00

14. *Conus rattus* Hwass. Indo-Pac. Syn: *C. tahitensis* Hwass. An olive-brown shell with a band of white on the body and another at the crown extending into the rounded spire. Purpled interior.
1¼″ .75

15. *Conus nussatella* L. P.I. Slim, with mottled white and brown markings and circled by numerous rings of small brown dots. The over-all look is a bit dull. 1½″—3″.
1¾″ 2.00

16. *Conus tessulatus* Born. Indo-Pac. Syn: *C. tessellatus* Hwass. Much variation in marking. The background is white, but the checkered squares or oblongs may be yellowish, peach-colored, orange, or orange-red. The colored tessellations also show on

Plate 20 (cont.)

the raised spire. The lower lip is often, but not always, tinged with violet.
$1\frac{1}{2}''$ 1.00

17. *Conus fulgetrum* Sow. Indo-Pac. Syn: *C. miliaris* Hwass. Pinkish, with circling lines and dots. Coronated. $1''$ .60

18. *Conus gradatus* Mawe. Panamic Prov. A member of a group of similar cones. Hanna and Strong suggest that it be distinguished from the others, all of which were once called *gradatus*, by its moderately high spire, larger size, and more extensive color arranged in "a series of large blotches, flammules and stripes." The whitish ground color forms a number of varying, indefinite spiral bands. $2''$ 1.50

19. *Conus catus* Hwass. P.I. Syn: *C. nubilis* Röd. Faintly bluish, with brown mottling. Lower half of body whorl has lines of raised dots or nodules. Spire is rounded and elevated. $1''$ .50

20. *Conus rosaceus* Chem. S.Afr. Bright orange, mottled with rose-white which almost appears as two indistinct bands. Rounded shoulders and a low spire. Specimens usually beach. Leading member of the *rosaceus* complex as classified by Turton in "The Marine Shells of Port Alfred." $1\frac{3}{4}''$ 1.40

21. *Conus spurius atlanticus* Clench. Fla. & W.I. Alphabet Cone. Syn: *Conus proteus* Hwass. Very variable markings which make up the broken orange rings on white sometimes resembling letters of the alphabet.

The similarly marked spire is channeled and rises to a sharp point. $1\frac{5}{8}''$ .75

22. *Conus litoglyphus* Hwass. Indo-Pac. Syns: *C. lithoglyphus* Lam. and *C. seychellensis* Nevill. A well-colored *litoglyphus* is an impressive-looking ornamental cone. It is a rich, glossy, orange-brown, tipped with black. The two very white, often wandering, bands are definite and do not invade the ground color. The top band is at the edge of the raised crown which is also mottled in white. Sometimes the white marks look like cryptic writing, and thus the shell's Latin name which means "engraving on a gem." $1\frac{3}{8}''$ 1.00

23. *Conus scabriusculus* Dillwyn. Pac. Syn: *C. fabula* Sow. Bluish white ground patched irregularly with brown. Broad shoulders rounding into a medium spire.
$1\frac{1}{4}''$ 3.50

24. *Conus victoriae* Reeve. N.Aust. Slightly plump, with a high spire and thin lip. Although the ground is white, only a little of it shows through the brownish lines which form a network of fine tenting. There are three indeterminate and broken brown bands. A subtly beautiful species.
$2''$ 1.50

25. *Conus infrenatus* Reeve. S.Afr. Pinkish white and brown bands, interrupted with dots of the contrasting color. Spire is almost flat with one deep ridge. A member of the *pictus* complex as arranged by Turton. See also No. 20 above. Specimens usually beach.
$1\frac{1}{2}''$ 1.20

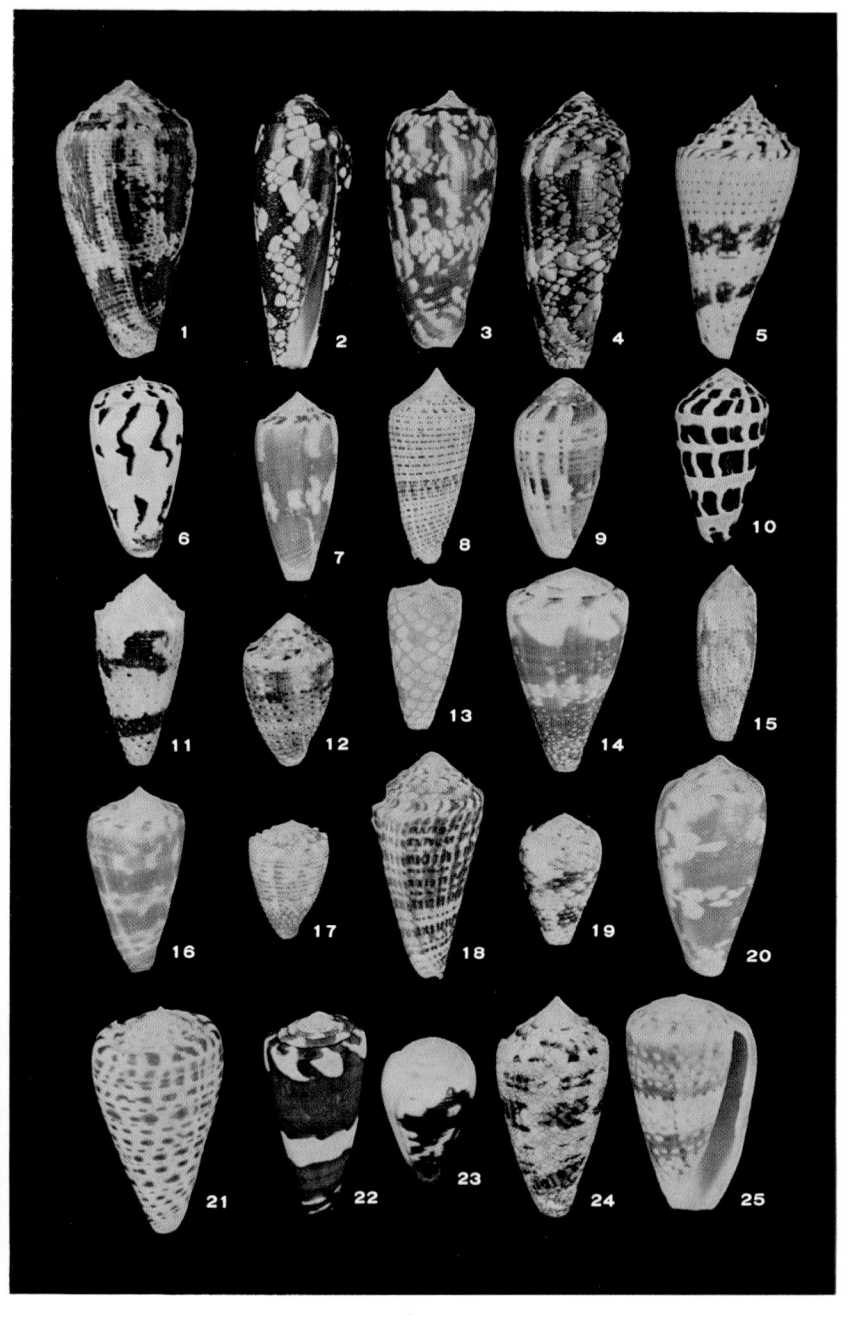

PLATE 20

Plate 21

1. *Conus sozoni* Bartsch. E.Mex. Yellow and brown markings and bandings. Sloped spire. Rare. See also Plate 17, No. 11.
2″ 10.00

2. *Terebra dimidiata* L. Indo-Pac. Salmon mottling on white. Secondary band on each whorl. To 6″.
3¼″ 1.25

3. *Terebra duplicata* L. E.Afr. Alternately ribbed whorls of light grey and dark brown.
2½″ .60

4. *Terebra taurina* Sol. W.I. to Fla. Syn: *T. flammea* Lam. Cloudy orange markings on white. Florida specimens scarce and expensive.
3¾″ 7.00

5. *Terebra chlorata* Lam. Indo-Pac. Two rows of blurred spots on each whorl.
2¾″ .75

6. *Terebra muscaria* Lam. Indo-Pac. Three rows of square brown spots on each whorl, and four on body whorl. Secondary ring distinguishes this from *T. subulata* L.
4″ 1.25

7. *Conus fulmen* Reeve. Japan. Brown mottling on faintly purplish white.
2¼″ 1.50

8. *Conus zonatus* Hwass. Maldive Is. Dark bandings and markings, sometimes resembling tents. Rare. See also Plate 53, No. 19.
2″ 26.00

9. *Conus vidua* Reeve. P.I. Widow Cone. White with dark mid and end bands. Tented. Rare form of *C. marmoreus* L.
2½″ 7.50

10. *Terebra strigata* Sow. Panamic Prov. Yellowish white, with strong, descending, dark stripes.
3½″ 1.50

11. *Terebra lanceata* L. Polynesia. White, with fine, descending, curved, brown lines.
1¼″ 1.00

12. *Terebra pretiosa* Reeve. Japan. Long and slender. Sculptured in wide and narrow bands. Wider bands scalloped. 2½″ .75

13. *Conus granulatus* L. W.I. Reddish. Granulated surface with circular ridges.

Indeterminate white bands. See also No. 18. Rare. 2¾″ Imperfect specimens 5.00

14. *Terebra triseriata* Gray. Aust. Brownish. Many whorls. Delicately slender. Scarce.
3½″ 3.50

15. *Terebra strigillata* Linné. P.I. Shiny grey-brown. Whorls edged by black dots on white.
2½″ 1.00

16. *Terebra robusta* Hinds. Panamic Prov. Two or more rows of brown or black spots or stripes.
3″ 1.25

17. *Conus vittatus* Hwass. Panamic Prov. Rib Bone Cone. Syn: *C. orion* Brod. Varies from white through orange and lilac to brown. Dark central band marked with white. Flame-shaped marks on spire. Not common.
1½″ 7.00

18. *Conus granulatus* L. W.I. Whitish specimen. See also No. 13.

19. *Terebra maculata* L. Indo. Pac. Marlin-Spike. Impressive and stocky. Brown squares and dots on cream. To 8″.
5″ 1.00

20. *Terebra guttata* Röd. P.I. Syn: *T. oculata* Lam. Salmon, with rings of white ovals. Incorrectly illustrated in some books. Rare.
3″ 2.50

21. *Terebra diversa* Smith. Japan. Grey, with black squares on spiral white bands.
1¼″ .50

22. *Terebra crenulata* L. Pac. Cream, ringed by brown dots and white knobs.
3″ 1.00

23. *Terebra hoffmeyeri* Abbott. P.I. A miniature. Shiny grey, with vertical ribs between whorls.
¾″ .50

24. *Terebra subulata* L. P.I. Cream, with two bars of squarish dark dots on edges of whorls. Distinguished by lack of secondary ring.
5″ 1.50

25. *Terebra tigrina* Gmel. Indo-Pac. Syn: *Terebra felina* Dillwyn. Light color, with circling brown dots.
1¾″ .75

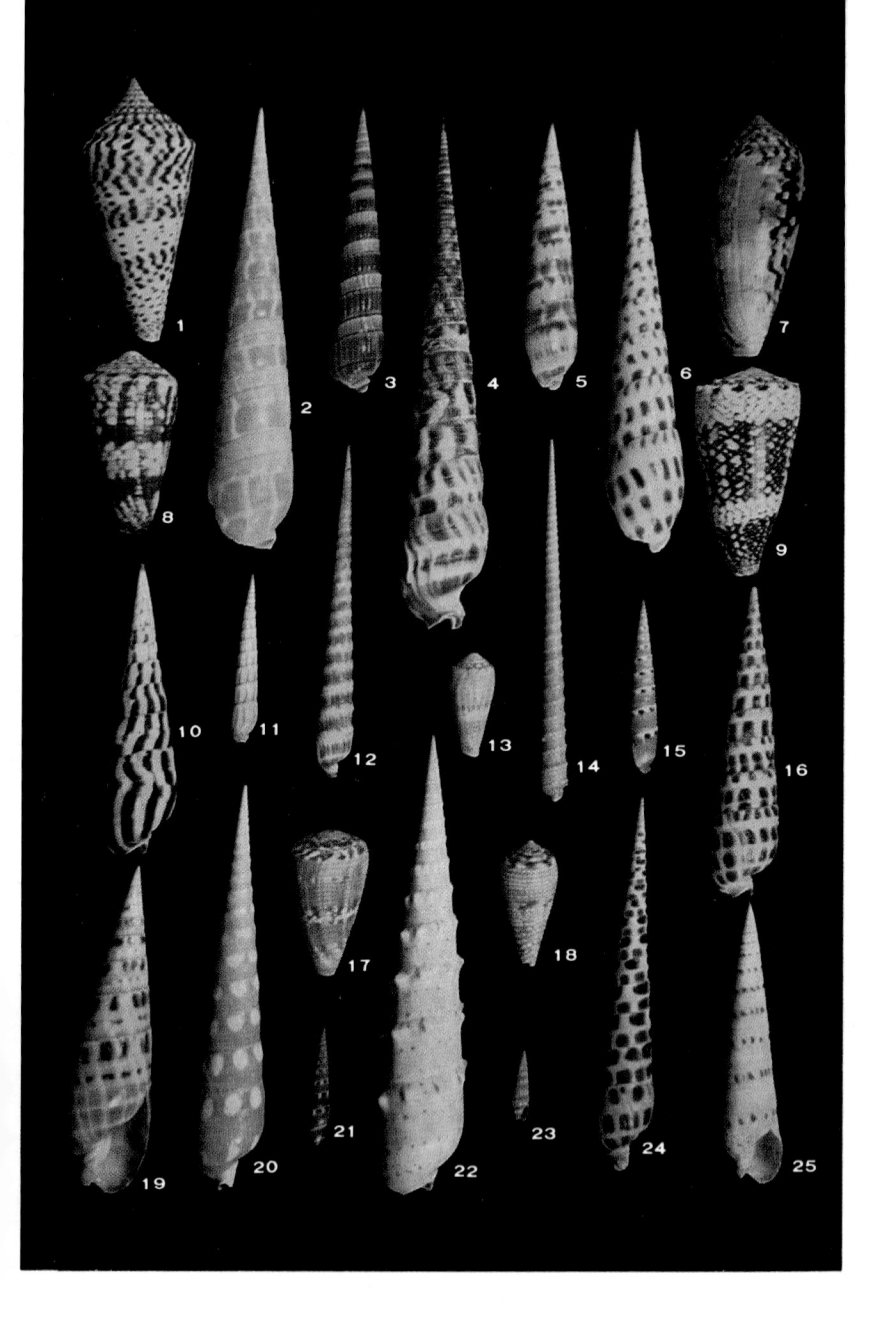

PLATE 21

Plate 22

1. *Pecten medius* Lam. Tasmania. Spectacular. Brown. White within.   4″ 1.25

2. *Pecten pes-felis* L. Sicily. Cat's Paw. Rare.   3″ 3.50 and up

3. *Pecten subnodosus* Sow. Panamic Prov. Largest of West Central American scallops. Cream, with more or less brown marking. Usually lime-coated. To 7″. Average large 5″. Cleaned 5.00, higher for special size, form, and color.

4. *Pecten maximus* L. Eng. Reddish. White inside. Largest of European scallops. To 5″.   3″ 1.00

5. *Pecten jacobeus* L. Sicily. Famous St. James Scallop or Pilgrim's Scallop. In popular thought associated with the Crusades. Fine sculpture.   4½″ 3.00

6. *Pecten excavatus* Anton. China. Syn: *P. sinensis* Sow. Brownish. One valve is concave; the other is deep-cupped even beyond wings.   3″ 2.50

7. *Pecten fulvicostatus* Ad. and Reeve. W. Aust. Yellow Rib. Uneven wings.   2″ 1.25

8. *Pecten larvatus* Reeve. Japan. Syn: *P. squamosus* Auch. Reddish, with scales.   1½″ 1.00

9. *Pecten nobilis* Reeve. Japan. Unequaled for color, the most prized being the oranges, the scarcer purples, and the rare lemon yellows. See also No. 15 and Plate 24, No. 7.   3½″ Orange 2.75

10. *Pecten pallium* L. P.I. Altar Cloth Pecten. A rich tapestry of purples embroidered with white.   2″ 1.25

11. *Pecten plica* L. Ceylon. Folded Scallop. Beautiful marbling of grey, brown, and white.   2¾″ 2.00

12. *Pecten squamatus* Gmel. Japan. Scales along colorful ribs frilling the edges.   2″ 1.50, higher for large and fine

13. *Pecten senatorius* Gmel. Indo-Pac. Syn: *P. miniaceus* Reeve. Color variations are brownish to startling red.   2¼″ 1.50 and up

14. *Pecten circularis* Sow. W.Mex. Fine color variations through white with streaks and patches to solid orange to purple. Inflated, with about 20 ribs.   Average 2″ .50, higher for fine color

15. *Pecten nobilis* Reeve. Japan. Purple. See also No. 9 and Plate 24, No. 7.   2½″ 2.25

16. *Pecten hirasei awajiensis* Pilsbry. Japan Shiny and mottled.   1¾″ 1.50

17. *Pecten purpuratus* Lam. Peru. Rose to purple coloring. To 6″.   2¼″ 1.00

18. *Pecten opercularis* L. French Coast. Sunset effect of orange and yellow.   2¼″ 1.50

19. *Pecten freieri akazara* Kuroda. Japan. Scaly ribs. This specimen has fine color.   1½″ 1.50, higher for fine color

20. *Pecten bifrons* Lam. Aust. White and purple, with purple inside.   2″ .75, 3″ 1.75

21. *Pecten caroli* Ired. Aust. Fine sculpture and ribbing. Red lines.   1½″ 1.25

PLATE 22

Plate 23

1. *Pecten swifti* Bernardi. Japan. A favorite. Often rose-purple above, and white with pinkish wings below. Raised ribs.
3¼″ Fine color 1.00

2. *Pecten patriae* Doello-Jurado. S.Coast Uruguay. From 90 fms. Delicate. Many red-orange radial ribs. White below.
2½″ 3.50

3. *Pecten laetus* Gould. Japan. Pink rings. Ribs with scalelike frills. Lower valve is mostly white.
2¾″ 1.00, higher for special color

4. *Pecten vexillum* Lam. P.I. This is an orange-colored variety of No. 5. Rare.
1½″ Orange 1.50

5. *Pecten vexillum* Lam. P.I.I. Like a Japanese fan, with its white clouds on black or brown.
1½″ .75

6. *Pecten zic-zac* L. W.I. to Venezuela. Upper valve is concave and purplish with fine zig-zag lines across ribs. Lower valve is convex, fluted, and pale lavender.
3″ Regular 2.00, Extra fine colors
10.00 and up

7. *Pecten glaber* L. Med.Sea. Smooth Scallop. Beautiful white patterning on grey. Raised ribs. White below.
1½″ .75

8. *Pecten scabriocostatus* Say. W.Aust. Orange to pink above and below. Ribs with scalelike frills. Rare.
2″ 1.50

9. *Pecten townsendi* Sow. Karachi, India. Reddish brown above and below. Scarce.
2″ 2.00

10. *Pecten gibbus* L. N.C. to W.I. Calico Scallop. Pink on white, with rings of dark markings across the ribs. White below.
1½″ .50

11. *Pecten heliacus* Dall. Fla. to W.I. White, with occasional radial orange rays

and with cross-mottling of purple-brown.
1½″ 1.50

12. *Pecten varius* L. Malta. Dark brown, with some faint light mottling.
1½″ 1.00

13. *Pecten gloriosus* Reeve. Queensland, Aust. Both valves are rough ribbed. Dark brown, with white near umbo. Ears of very uneven size. Not common.
1½″ 1.00, bright colors 2.00

14. *Pecten sericeus* Hinds. W.Mex. Brown to pink. About 22 crinkled ribs. Upper valve is concave, and lower one is convex and brightly colored. Rare. 2½″ 7.50

15. *Pecten funebris* Reeve. N.W.Aust. Orange color variety shown. Ears not even.
1¾″ 1.50

16. *Pecten convexus* Q. & G. N.Zealand. Found in deep water. Ears are uneven. About five raised and many fine radial ribs. Pink shading on white. White below. Rare.
1⅝″ 3.00

17. *Pecten raveneli* Dall. Gulf of Mex. Ears are even. Upper valve is concave, and lower one is convex. Sometimes well-colored in browns to pinks.
2″ 2.50 and up

18. *Pecten lividus* Lam. N.S.W., Aust. Syn: *P. tegula* Wood. Upper valve is brown on yellow, with strong rough frilling along ribs. Flatter and yellowish below. Uneven ears. Not common. 2¼″ 1.50

19. *Pecten alba* Tate. Tasmania. Brown to orange, with strong rounded fluting. Exterior of one valve flat, of the other convex. Below is yellowish with broader fluting. Ears even. 3½″ 2.00

20. *Pecten tigris* Lam. Pac. White, with tiger mottling in brown above. Mottled white below. Asymmetrical valves. Strong fluting and fine ribbing. Not common.
2″ 1.50

PLATE 23

Plate 24

1. *Pecten nodosus* L. N.C. to Venezuela. Rare orange specimen. See also No. 5 and No. 11. Rare color varieties or unusually knobbed. 2¼″—3¼″ 10.00—30.00 and up

2. *Spondylus varians* Sow. Polynesia. Heavy and thick. Fine beardlike spines. This specimen is pink against white. One valve is convex. Umbo prominent. 5″ 8.00

3. *Pecten maximus* L. Eng. Upper valves flat. Brown, with mottling. White even wings. Lower valve is convex. White to cream. 3″ 1.00

4. *Spondylus avicularis* (?) Lam. W.I. Names in this genus are unsettled. Coarse, heavy, and thick. Cream, touched with pink to yellow. To 10″. 6″ 4.00

5. *Pecten nodosus* L. Fla. This specimen is of rare color and quality. See also No. 1 and No. 11.
2¼″—3¼″ 10.00—30.00 and up

6. *Spondylus americanus* Lam. Fla. This is a fine color variety. To 8″ 5.00—20.00 and up, depending on color and quality. See also Plate 25, No. 2.

7. *Pecten nobilis* Reeve. Japan. Perhaps the brightest colored of all sea shells. A series showing its spectrum can be brilliant. This specimen is a very rare red. See also Plate 22, Nos. 9 and 15. 5″ 8.00 and up

8. *Amusium japonicum* Gmel. Japan. Thin and orb-like. The mahogany color of the upper valve contrasts strongly with the yellow ribbed or toothed edges of the inside of the white lower valve. 4½″ 1.00

9. *Pecten caurinus* Gould. Vancouver. This huge orbicular fragile scallop is rich brown with beautifully radiating ribs. The lower valve overlaps, showing an edge of the interior white. Good unbroken specimens scarce. 6″ 3.50

10. *Cardium pseudolima* Lam. E.Afr. Grand and globular, with neat pleatlike ribs. 5″ 5.00

11. *Pecten nodosus* L. N.C. to Venezuela. Lion's Paw. This unusual specimen, with 99 knobs, is the typical color, purple-brown. This shell ranges through cream and yellow to orange. Usually dredged in 10 to 20 fms. Becoming scarcer. See also No. 1 and No. 5. Florida specimens of typical color and ordinary knobbing 2¼″—6″ 3.50—16.00, according to size and quality. Rare color varieties, orange and yellow, 2¼″—3¼″ 10.00—30.00 and up, according to size, color quality, and knobs.

12. *Cardium elatum* Sow. W.Mex. A graceful yellow globe, with fine yellow ribs crossed by gracefully curving bands. Probably the largest and heaviest of the genus. 5″ 3.00

PLATE 24

Plate 25

1. *Spondylus gussoni* DaCosta. Gulf of Mex. Red Thorny Oyster. Shades of red. Few spines. 2½″ 3.00

2. *Spondylus americanus* Lam. Gulf of Mex. Eastern Thorny Oyster. Magnificent variations in size, spines, and color of white through red. See also Plate 24, No. 6. Small 2½″ to 3″ specimens have slender spines. Larger specimens may have stubby ones. From 10 to 12 fms. To 8″ 5.00—20.00 and up, according to size and quality

3. *Spondylus imperialis* Chem. Aust. Imperial Thorny Oyster. From 8 to 12 fms. 3″ 6.00 and up

4. *Spondylus barbatus* Reeve. Japan. Japanese Thorny Oyster. Color variations through white and brown to purple. Broad short spines. 3″ 1.00

5. *Spondylus butleri* Reeve. P.I. Inside cupped under hinge. White to brown, orange, or purple. 3½″ 5.00

6. *Spondylus foliaceus* Chem. Pac. Wide, radiating, purplish red ribs. Spines fernlike at ends. Valves are deep-cupped and usually lime-coated. 2½″ 3.00

7. *Spondylus regius* L. Japan. Royal Thorny Oyster. Superb. Purple to bright orange or red. Smaller ones may have longer spines. Not common. 5″ 15.00, best to 25.00 and up, according to size, color, and quality

8. *Spondylus ducalis* Bolten. P.I. Radiating blackish and white lines. White ribs with short spines. Usually lime-coated. 2″—3″ 1.00—2.50, according to quality

9. *Spondylus tenellus* Crosse. Aust. Usually delicate shades of pink on white. Many fine sharp spines. 3″ 3.50

10. *Spondylus princeps* Brod. W.Mex. Syns: *S. pictorum* Sow. and *S. crassisquamatus* Lam. Bright colors in variations of white rose, salmon, orange, or red. Scarce. 2″—6″ 3.50—15.00 and up, according to quality

11. Same as No. 10.

Plate 26

1. *Cardium cardissa* L. P.I. Syn: *Corculum cardissa* L. Yellow. There are some variety names based on color, but these are not reliable. See also No. 2. 1¼″—2¼″ .50—2.50, according to size and color

2. *Cardium cardissa* L. P.I. Red dots. See also No. 1. 1¼″ 1.50

3. *Pecten hericeus* Gould. Puget Sound, U.S.A. Pink Scallop. Red banding on orange. Thin. Color varies. 2¾″ 1.00

4. *Trochus radiata* Gmel. N.Queensland, Aust. Top-shaped. Red mottling on white. 1¼″ × 1½″ high .50

5. *Pecten hindsi* Dall. Puget Sound, U.S.A. Delicate. Usually pale pink. Yellow is scarce. *Pecten hindsi navarchus* Dall is lavender and rarer. 2″ .60, yellow 1.25

6. *Mitra caffra* L. P.I. Glossy, dark, and ringed by light yellow bands. 2″ 1.25

7. *Cantharidus opalis* Mart. N.Zealand. Mottling in white and brown descending waves. Inside is opalescent. 1¼″ 1.25

8. *Cymatium tenuiliratum* Lisch. Japan. Brownish. Slim, with fine cross-ribbing. 2″ 1.50

9. *Tudicula armigera* A. Adams. Aust. Stout body whorl. Long canal. Spiny. Quality varies. Rare. 2½″ 4.50

10. *Cardium unedo* L. P.I. Yellowish to cream. Handsomely marked with red-brown scales across ribs. 2¼″ 1.00

11. *Pecten spectibilis* Reeve. New Caledonia. Upper valve is light brown, with fluted ribs crossed by squares of white and black in striking pattern. Not common. 1″ 2.00

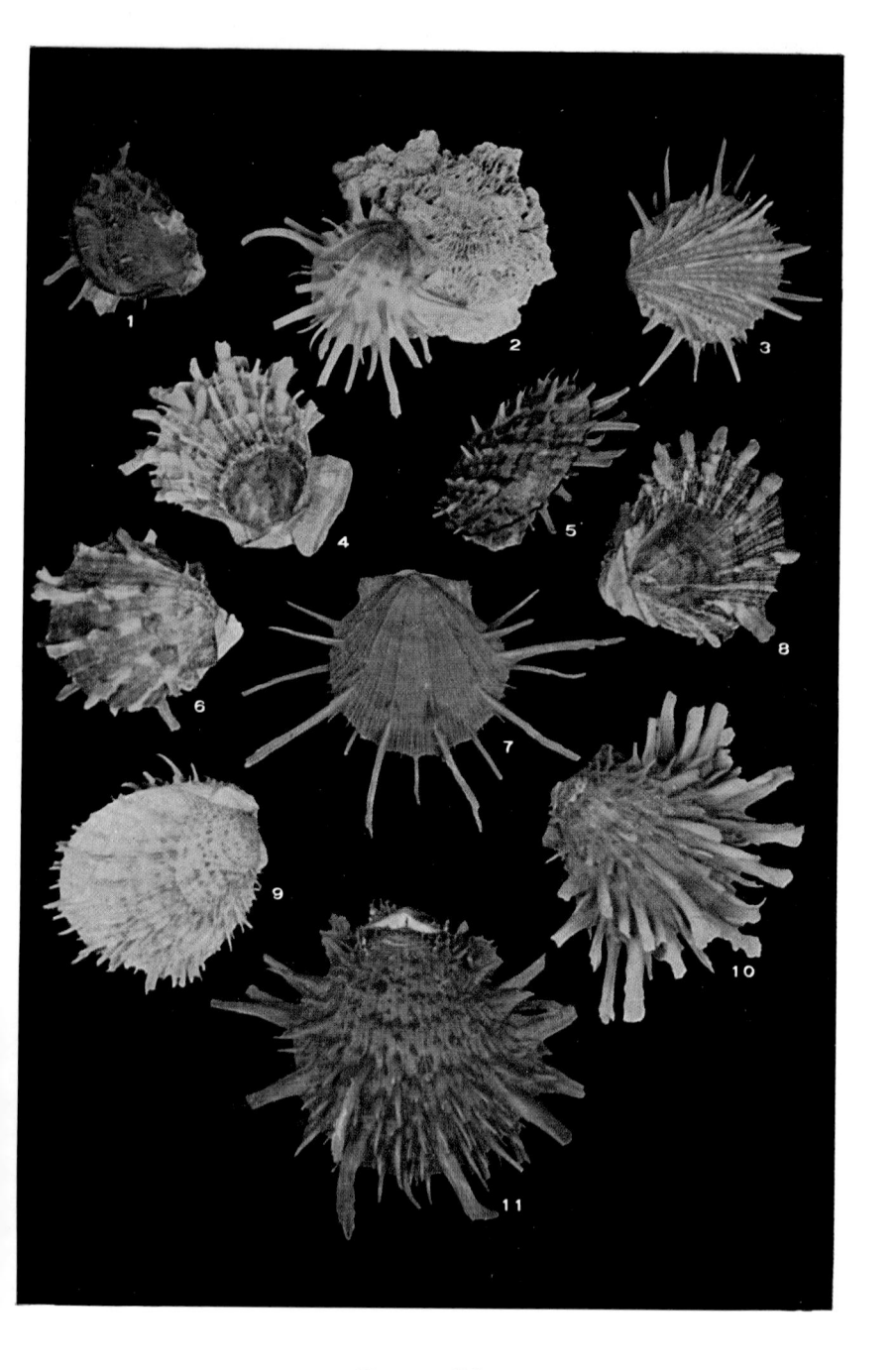

PLATE 25

Plate 26 (cont.)

12. *Pecten cristalaris* Ad. & Reeve. Hong Kong. Flat ribs. Shades of red. 1″ 1.25

13. *Pecten muscosus* Wood. Gulf of Mex. Syn: *P. exasperatus* Sow. Bright orange-red, with extended wings and fine scaling. 1¾″ Rare color 10.00

14. *Northia northiae* Griffith & Pidgeon. Panamic Prov. Olive brown. Shiny. Neat sculpture. High spire. Saw lip. Not common. 2″ 1.00

15. *Pecten asperrimus* Lam. S.E.Aust. Prickly Scallop. Light weight. About 30 main ribs with fine spiny scales. Color varies from yellow to vivid reds, browns, and purples. Unequal ears. Fine color forms. 3″ 2.50

16. *Cassis (Casmaria) turgida* Rve., Indo-Pac. Smooth with high spire, 6—12 sharp denticles on outer lip. Color varies from cream to ash and brown. Longitudinal brown flames. Columellar area twisted. 2″—3″ 2¼″ .75

17. *Donax serra* Chem. S.Afr. Yellow to pink. Purplish inside. Saw edge. 2¼″ .75

18. *Murex territus* Ired. Aust. Varices almost winged. Saw teeth on lip. 1¾″ 6.00

19. *Voluta (Amoria) canaliculata* McCoy. Aust. White. Interrupted descending orange lines. Rare. 1¾″ 10.00 and up

20. *Voluta (Ternivoluta) studeri* von Martens. E.Aust. Cream, with descending fine yellowish lines and faint yellow banding. Whorls of spire set back in a concave platform. Shell is shiny and semi-translucent. 2″ 4.50

21. *Voluta (Aulicina) nivosa* Lam. W. Aust. Grey-white, with some faint banding. Creases in whorls of nucleus. Nodules on shoulder. Four plaits, three oblique and one descending. Rare. 2″ 4.50

22. *Voluta (Cymbiolacca) complexa* Ired. Queensland, Aust. Syn: *Voluta punctata* Swain. Pinkish brown with darker flecks and faint banding. Nodules on shoulder and spire. Four plaits. Rare. 2¼″ 12.00

23. *Voluta (Amoria) turneri* Gray. Aust. Cream, with brown lines and mottling in two bands. Rare. 2″ 5.00

24. *Murex espinosus* Macpherson. Queensland, Aust. Stout varices, a short spined canal, and spines on lip. 2¼″ 5.00

25. *Cardium lyratum* Sow. Indo-Pac. Globose. Notable for maroon-red color and ribbing in two directions. 2¼″ 1.50

26. *Voluta (Aulica) flavicans* Gmel. S.W. Aust. Syns: *V. tissotiana* Crosse and *V. quaesita* Ired. White-to-cream elongated ovate. Thick. Varies much from faint to dark brown markings. Rare. See Plate 42, No. 1. 2½″ 6.00 and up

27. *Voluta (Aulicina) norrisi* Grey, 1838. Solomon Islands and Aust. Syns: *V. piperita* Sow, 1844 and *V. ceraunia* Crosse, 1880. Complicated patterns of grey and brown banding on cream. Aperture is pink-orange. 3″ 5.00

28. *Neptunea decemcostata* Say. N.S. to Mass. Brownish. Strikingly ribbed with low brown keels spiraling body whorl. 2¾″ Best 2.00

29. *Cancellaria cassidiformis* Sow. W.Mex. Brown, with a white band. Parietal callus. See also Plate 42, No. 10. 1¼″ 1.25

30. *Pecten magellanicus* Gmel. Newfoundland to New Engl. Atlantic Deep Sea Scallop. Syn: *P. grandis* Sol. Almost circular. Red-brown, paling to pink. Lower valve is pinkish white and almost flat. Scarce because shells are always shucked and discarded at sea during deep-sea dredging. 4″ 1.50

31. *Voluta (Amoria) damoni* Gray. Aust. Syn: *V. reticulata* Reeve. Cream, with brown network mostly in three bands. Resembles *V. keatsiana* Ludbrook, but spire has a light angular band. Rare. 3″ 7.00 and up

32. *Cardium bechei* Reeve. Japan. Silken red-brown. Cross-ribbing at side with sharp scales. 1½″ 1.50

33. *Pecten irradians irradians* Lam. N.S. to N.Y. Bay Scallop. Usually mottled grey-brown, but fine color variations occur. Scarce color variations are orange and black, cream and yellow, or cream and white with dark marks. Scarcest is black with white stripes. 2¾″ according to color .50—1.50

PLATE 26

Plate 27

1. *Chama macerophylla* Gmel. Fla. to W.I. Jewel Box. Bivalve with yellow or purple fronds. 2″—3″ 2.50—5.00

2. *Tellina virgata* L. Indo-Pac. Yellow and red rays. 2″ .60

3. *Chama exogyra* Conrad. Calif. Translucent. Foliated with fine fronds. 2″ Fine 1.00

4. *Tellina perieri* Bertin. Japan. Pink Winged Tellin. Fragile. Strong pink color. 2″ .60

5. *Crassatella gibbosa* Sow. W.Mex. Cinnamon brown. Distinguished by size and pointed posterior end. 2½″ 1.50

6. *Glycymeris suipta* Born. W.Afr. Pinkish, with thin brown lines in leaflike patterns. 2″ 3.00

7. *Glycymeris vovan* Lamy. W.Afr. Redbrown. Circular, and almost globular. About 19 teeth on hinge. 2″ 3.00

8. *Lioconcha castrensis* L. P.I. Cream, with unique branching V-markings. 1½″ 1.25

9. *Cardita laticostata* Sow. Panamic Prov. Almost rectangular. About three squareedged ribs. Light brown, with waving bands of white. 1¾″ .60

10. *Callanaitis disjecta* Perry. S.E.Aust. Syn: *Venus lamellata* Lam. The unique Pastry Shell. White with about six unusual high frills which gracefully converge to a point and bend. 1¾″—2½″ 1.50—3.00

11. *Venus (Tivela) byronensis* Gray. W. Mex. Brownish, with white circles and rays in very variable patterns. Identifiable by a spot of dark blue in the beaks. 1½″ .50

12. *Pitar roseus* Brod. & Sow. Panamic Prov. Alternating concentric ridges in cream and rose. Spiny ridge on posterior umbonal angle. 2″ 1.50

13. *Circe divaricatum* Gmel. P.I. Circular, with brown V's, Y's, or W's on white, which may suggest imaginary pictures. 1¼″ .50

14. *Austromactra caloundra* Ired. N.S.W. & N.Aust. Bluish. Usually blue-violet concentric bands, and violet inside. 1½″ 1.00

15. *Cardium lyratum* Sow. P.I. Deep red, tending to white at the umbonal surface. Surface lines in two directions. Scarce. 2¼″ 1.50

16. *Semele purpurascens* Gmel. Gulf of Mex. Purple V's and W's in concentric circles on white. 1¼″ 2.00

17. *Circe scripta* L. P.I. Concentric ridges Brown V's and W's on white. 2″ .75

18. *Venus (Cyclina) sinensis* Gmel. Japan. Circular. Coffee color, edged with purple. 1¾″ .50

19. *Tellina rastellum* Hanley. Mozambique. Yellow rays. Concentric bands of purplish red. 3¼″ 1.00

20. *Cardium cardissa* L. P.I. A series is needed to show this unique heart-shaped favorite. Very variable, it ranges through white, cream, and yellow, often with pink marking, edging, or polka dots. One side is concave; the other is convex. 1¼″—2¼″ .50—2.50

21. *Cardium bechei* Reeve. Japan. Silky. Light brown to pink at umbos. Heartshaped side is lined with rough ridges. Scarce. 1½″ 1.50

22. *Tapes turgida* Lam. N.Aust. Almost rectangular, with concentric ridges. Cream, flecked with deep brown. 2¼″ .75

23. *Trachycardium belcheri* Brod. & Sow. Panamic Prov. Superb coloration in pastel shades of yellow, rose, and orange-brown. Globose. Twenty to twenty-five saw-tooth ridges on each valve. Deep water. Rare. 2″ 2.50

PLATE 27

Plate 28

1. *Neptunea pribiloffensis* Dall. Puget Sound to Alaska. Yellowish. Flaring cream lip. Circled by narrow tan bands which are slightly raised and more prominent on shoulder. Fragile. Named for Pribiloff Islands of Bering Sea.   4½″ 2.00

2. *Neptunea phoenicius* Dall. Puget Sound to S. Alaska. Medium brown, with lighter lip and columella. Small raised lines circling entire shell, lines tending to whitish above body whorl.   3½″ 3.00

3. *Neptunea lyrata* Gmel. Calif. to Alaska. Tan ridges encircling entire shell. Interior of lip is peach color. Solid. Lip flares less than that of *N. pribiloffensis.* 4½″ 2.00

4. *Neptunea smirnia* Dall. Alaska to Wash. Dark brown. Paler in lip. Often with growth mends.   3″ 4.00

5. *Neptunea tabulata* Baird. Brit.Colum. to San Diego. White to cream. Semi-fragile and perhaps semi-translucent. The neat tabled whorls of the spire and the graceful whorls produce a very distinguished form. "A choice collector's item."   3″ 3.50

6. *Distorsio reticulata* Röd. Japan. Brown. Enameled on flaring lip and on wide columella area. Twisted appearance is due to varied depth of spiral whorls. Circular spirals cross descending ribs to form a network. White denticulation all about the opening.   2½″ 1.00

7. *Argobuccinum murrayi* Smith. S.Afr. White. Lip flares downward. Many cross-reticulations. Varices absent or residual. Short recurved canal.   3½″ 2.00

8. *Argobuccinum oregonensis* Redfield. San Diego to Bering Sea. Removal of hairy periostracum shows white shell with faint brown spirals crossing vertical ribbing. Single tooth near top of aperture.
    4″ 1.25

9. *Patella mexicana* Brod. & Sow. Panamic Prov. Thick and heavy. Rough exterior and smooth white interior. Largest living limpet. Said to reach 14″, but usually 4″—6″.
    6″ 1.50, 8″ 3.00

10. *Bursa gigantea* Lam. Med.Sea. Syn *Ranella gigantea* Lam. Brownish. Circling nodulated ribs. Two varices to each whorl advancing one position on each whorl Aperture is white. Notch at top. Dentules in columella. Canal recurved.   4½″ 4.00

PLATE 28

Plate 29

1. *Voluta (Halia) priamus* Gmel. Canary Is. Swollen. Pale brown, circled by darker bands and with rows of squarish dots. Very rare. 2½″ 18.00

2. *Cominella elongata Dunker.* S.Afr. 1¾″ 1.00

3. *Lotorium nodifer* Lam. S.Afr. 1½″ .50

4. *Babylonia papillaris* Sow. S.Afr. 1½″ .80

5. *Epitonium (Amaea) teremachii* Kuroda. Japan. See also No. 33. 1½″ 3.00

6. *Epitonium perplexum* Pease. Japan. Brown line on body whorl. ⅝″ 1.00

7. *Epitonium (Amaea) thielei* De Boury. Japan. 1¼″ .50

8. *Cominella delalandei* Gould. S.Afr. 1¼″ .50

9. *Nassarius filmerae* Sow. S.Afr. Brownish. See also No. 23. ¾″ .30

10. *Epitonium (Amaea) tertitum* Kuroda. Japan. 1½″ 2.25

11. *Epitonium nitidum* Kuroda. Japan. ½″ 2.25

12. *Epitonium (Amaea) splendidum* De Boury. Japan. 1½″ 2.50

13. *Turritella carinifera* Lam. S.Afr. 2½″ .45

14. *Ancilla fasciata* Reeve. S.Afr. Syn: *A. albozonata* Sow. ¾″ .60

15. *Marginella ornata* Redfield. S.Afr. 1⅛″ .75

16. *Bullia callosa* Wood. S.Afr. 1¾″ .90

17. *Ancilla reevei* Smith. S. Afr. ⅝″ .50

18. *Latiaxis fritchi* Smith. S.Afr. ⅝″ 1.50

19. *Epitonium zelebori* Dunker. N.Zealand. ⅝″ .60

20. *Epitonium pyramidalis* Kuroda. Japan. ⅝″ 1.50

21. *Epitonium coronatum* Lam. S.Afr. 1⅛″ 1.25

22. *Turritella kowiensis* Sow. S.Afr. ⅝″ .35

23. *Nassarius filmerae* Sow. S.Afr. See also No. 9. ¾″ .30

24. *Mitra aerumbosa* Melvill. S.Afr. 1¼″ .75

25. *Bullia digitalis* Meusch. S.Afr. 1⅝″ .50

26. *Mitra picta* Reeve. S.Afr. 1⅜″ .75

27. *Epitonium auritum* Sow. Japan. ⅜″ .35

28. *Epitonium japonicum* Dunker. Japan. ⅜″ .75

29. *Turritella knysnaensis* Sow. S.Afr. 1″ .35

30. *Bullia rhodostoma* Reeve. S.Afr. 1¼″ .50

31. *Melatoma kraussi* Smith. S.Afr. 1″ .50

32. *Murex uncinarius* Lam. S.Afr. ½″—1″. 1″ 1.00

33. *Epitonium (Amaea) teramachii* Kuroda. Japan. See also No. 5. 1″ 1.50

34. *Epitonium stigmaticum* Pilsbry. Japan. 1″ 2.00

35. *Epitonium (Clathroscala) tosaensis* Kuroda. Japan. 1″ 2.25

36. *Hydatina physis* L. S. Afr. 1″ 1.25

37. *Melatoma sybaritica* Bartsch. S. Afr. 1″ .40

38. *Thais squamosa* Lam. S.Afr. 1½″ .40

39. *Melatoma rosaria* Reeve. S.Afr. 1¼″ .40

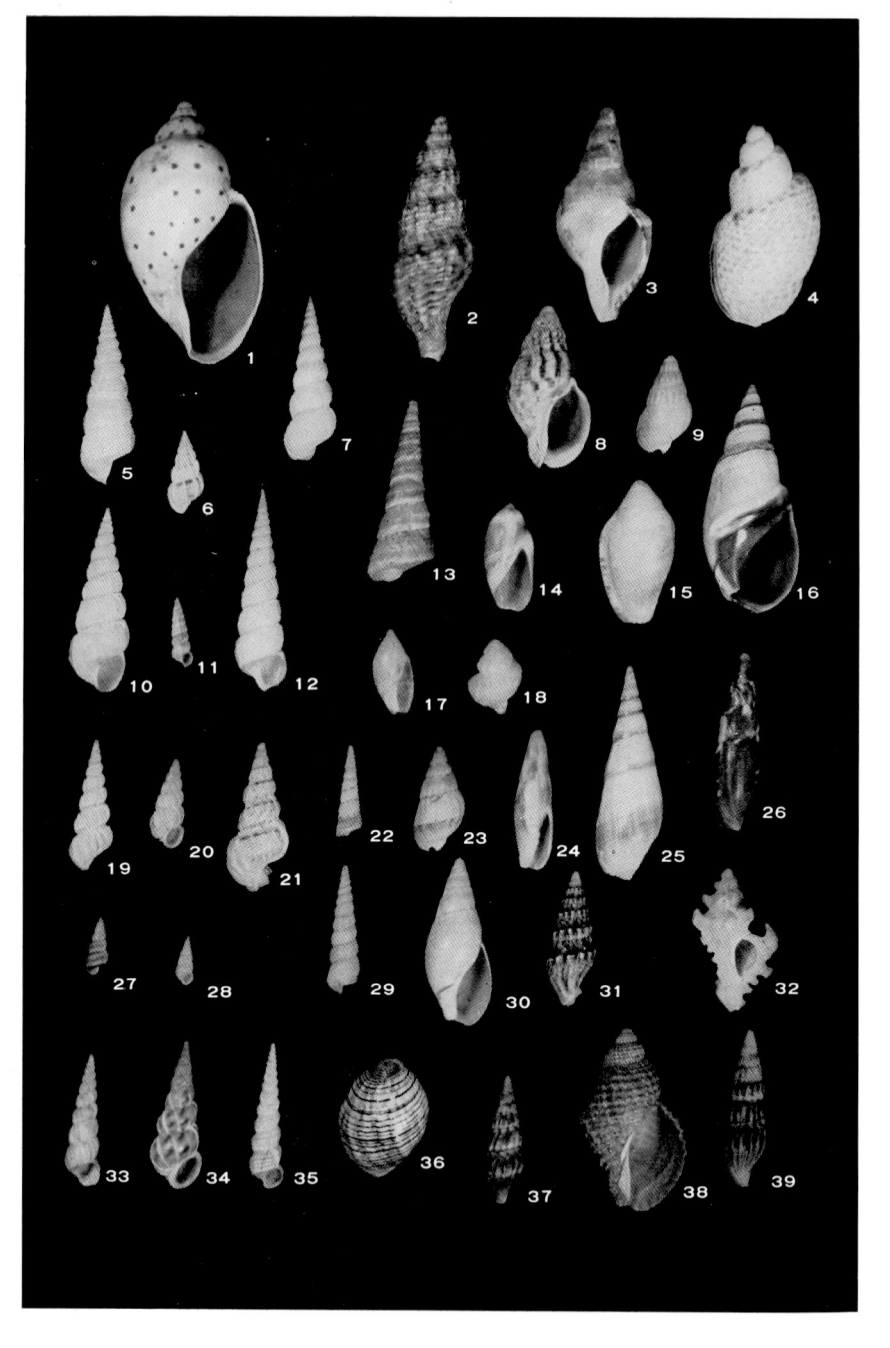

PLATE 29

Plate 30

1. *Astraea rotularia* Lam. N.W.Aust. White. Spiraling frill of foldlike formations. 1¼″ 1.75

2. *Murex (Ceratostoma) japonicus* Dunker. Japan, Puget Sound, & Wash. Grey-white. Varices and cross-ribs. Outer lip thick, and inner lip reflected. A Japanese mollusk introduced into Puget Sound. 1½″ .75

3. *Acmaea fenestrata cribraria* Gould. Alaska to N.Calif. Dark interior. One lighter ring. ⅞″ .25

4. *Cymatium gutternium* Röd. E.Aust. White to buff. Ribbed up and down and across. Long slender canal. 2″ 1.00

5. *Astraea americana* Gmel. Fla. Keys & W.I. White. Rings of nodes. Descending ridges. White dimpled operculum. 1″ .35

6. *Murex hirasei* Hirase. Japan. Brown, with fine circling brown lines. Long canal. Thorny spines in varices. 1½″ 5.00

7. *Cuspidaria hirasei* Kuroda. Japan. White, with a keeled canal typically extended. 1¼″—1½″. 1¼″ 1.25

8. *Cuspadaria suganumai* Nomura. Japan. White. Canal produced. 1¼″ .75

9. *Murex (Ceretostoma) modestum* Fulton. Japan. Light brown. Triangular appearance. 1¼″ 1.00

10. *Protothaca staminea* Conrad. Puget Sound. Rock Venus. Whitish, often with brown chevrons. Radiating lines cross concentric ones. Marketed for food. 2″—2½″. 2″ .35

11. *Colus australis* Q. and G. Barrier Reef, Aust. White. Swollen tips on upper part but not on body whorl. Slender. Canal about one half length of shell. 5½″ 1.50

12. *Tegula funebralis* A Adams Oregon & Calif. Black Turban. Black, with pearl under-layer. Two small knobs at base of columella. 1″ .25

13. *Botula falcata* Gould. Oregon to San Diego. Pea Pod. Fragile blue elongated bivalve. Bores a home in solid rock from which specimens are chiseled. 2½″ .60

14. *Latiaxis winckworthi* Fulton. Japan. White. Shoulder spines. Varices crossed by circling lines and fine nodules. Deeply unbilicated. 1½″ 5.00

15. *Thais lamellosa* Gmel. Alaska to Calif. Wrinkled Thais. Wide bands of white and brown. Color variable. Smooth or with frilled varices. 2″ .50

16. *Voluta (Saotomea) delicata* Fulton. Japan. Pinkish grey. Spindle-shaped. Ribbed on upper half. 1¾″ 1.00

17. *Acmaea scabra* Gould. West U.S.A. Rough Limpet. White inside, with brown at center. 1″ .25

18. *Acmaea patina* Eschscholtz. Alaska to Calif. Plate Limpet. Outer ring of squares around inner patch of dark brown. Bluish white interior. Variable. 1¼″ .35

19. *Acmaea limatula* Carp. Puget Sound to Mex. File Limpet. Shiny bluish white interior. Brown outer ring around patch. 1″ .25

20. *Acmaea pelta* Esch. Bering Sea to Mex. Shield Limpet. High and conical. About 25 descending wedges of dark on white. Inside is white. 1½″ .35

21. *Haliotis cyclobates* Péron. W.Aust. Round-Back Ear Shell. Syn: *H. excavata* Lam. Body whorl is most of shell, but small high spire. Interior is deep and iridescent. 2″ 1.25

22. *Thais emarginata* Deshayes. Bering Sea to S. Calif. Variable from squat to elongated. Circling lighter and darker lines. Like East Coast *Thais lapillus* L. 1″ .25

23. *Acmaea digitalis* Esch. Aleutians to Mex. Fingered Limpet. Radial digitations. 1″ .35

24. *Cypraea pallidula rhinoceros* Souverbie. S.W.Pac. Pale and faintly banded. Small light-brown freckles. Posteriorly umbilicated. 1″ 2.50

25. *Astraea pileola* Reeve. N.W.Aust. White. Frills form a rosette. 1¾″ 1.25

PLATE 30

Plate 31

1. *Tonna sulcosa* Born. Pac. Syn: *T. fasciata* Brug. White, with wide brown bands. Circled by ribs and channels. Black nucleus. 2″—5″. 4¼″ 2.00

2. *Conus elisae* Kien. E.Afr. Finely netted or tented. Descending blue lines. Dark bands. Rare. 2″ 8.00

3. *Tonna luteostoma* Küster. Japan. Thin and light. The neatly molded ribs are marked alternately with squarish white and brown patches. Channels show through on inside lip. 2½″—4¼″ .50—1.00

4. *Tonna allium* Dillwyn. Pac. Syn: *T. costata* Deshayes. White. Thin yellowish spiral ribs separated by white channels. Descending pleat. Brown nucleus. 2¼″ .75

5. *Xancus laevigatus* Anton. Brazil. White, with brown periostracum. Elongated, bulbous, heavy body whorl. Spire slims to nucleus. Three platelike plaits on smooth white columella. Scarce. 4½″ 3.75

6. *Cassis (Morum) cancellata* Sow. Japan. White, with brown shading and banding. Descending ribs with many sharp nodules. The white columella is granulose. Rare. 1½″ 3.50

7. *Cassis (Semicassis) bulla* Kuroda. Japan. Thin and inflated. Shiny, translucent beige. Twisted canal. 2″ .75

8. *Cassis (Casmaria) cernica* Sow. Japan. Thin, shiny, and semi-translucent. Light brown banding on beige. Dark patches on raised lip. Canal is twisted. 2″ .65

9. *Cassis (Eudolium) pyriformis* Sow. Japan. Fine banding and channeling. Brown patching on cream. Lavender lip. 2¼″ 1.25

10. *Cassis (Eudolium) lineata inflata* Kuroda & Habe. Japan. Cream, ringed with lines of brown nodulose hyphens. Nucleus is brown. Teeth on lip. 1¾″ 2.75

11. *Tonna pomum* L. Pac. Shiny, with rounded ribs and channels crossed by gray, brown, and white. Ribbed teeth on yellowish columella and lip. 1½″—3″. 1¾″ .50

12. *Cassis (Semicassis) pfefferi* Hidalgo. Japan. White, with fine cross-ribbing and bands of brown squares. Pleated lip. 1½″ .25

13. *Tonna tessellata* Lam. Japan. Thin, globose, white. Rounded ribs with alternating oblongs of brown and white. Wide aperture. 2½″—4″ .75—2.00

14. *Tonna chinensis* Dillwyn. Japan. Varying coloration of browns to blue-grey, and white. Bandings of light brown. Descending lines made by pairs of dark squares. 2″ 1.00

15. *Tonna olearia* L. Pac. Syn: *T. cepa* Röd., 1798. Thin and globose. Bands of brown paralleled by fine paired or tripled channels of grey-lavender. Spire is whitish with deep-cut sutures. 3″—8″. 7″ 5.00

Plate 32

1. *Architectonica trochlearis* Hinds. Japan. Light brown, with spiral brown line at suture. Flat, but umbilicus deep, with circling brown teeth. Spirals of neat brown squares. 1½″—2¾″ .75—3.00

2. *Architectonica acutissima* Sow. Japan. Acutely flat. Light brown with paler spiral. Umbilicus almost to spire. 1½″ 3.00

3. *Architectonica maxima* Philippi. Japan. Light brown. Spiraling white line in suture. Flat, but umbilicus deep, with spiraling white teeth. Indefinitely-formed spiraling squares. 1½″—2¾″ .75—3.00

4. *Stomatella imbricata* Lam. Aust. Sand-colored. Spiraling striae. Wide aperture. Inside is pearl. 1¼″ .50

PLATE 31

Plate 32 (cont.)

5. *Pyrene philippinarum* Recluz. P.I. Syn: *Columbella philippinarum* Recluz. Surprisingly handsome. White, with waving dark brown marking.   3/4″   .25

6. *Pyrene strombiformis* Lam. Gulf of Calif. Syn: *Columbella s.* Attractive markings. Top of lip is angled.   1″   .50

7. *Solidula solidula* L. Indo-Pac. Neatly cylindrical. Circled by broken dark lines.   1″   .35

8. *Bursa ranelloides* Reeve. Japan. Brown on darker brown. Yellowish color on apertural nodes.   2″   .50

9. *Cymatium tenuiliratum* Lisch. Japan. Pale brown, fine ridges cross the swollen varices, and fan-out at lip.   2″   1.50

10. *Dentalium crocinum* Dall. Japan. Peach color. Has varnished look.   2½″   1.00

11. *Dentalium aprinum* L. P.I. Green-grey. Fluted.   2½″   1.00

12. *Dentalium weinkauffi* Dunker. Japan. Peach color or white. Smooth.   3¼″   .75

13. *Dentalium elephantinum* L. P.I. Dark green, which lightens to white. Ribbed.   3″   1.00

14. *Dentalium vernedei* Sow. Japan. White, with yellow banding. Many close-set ribs.   4″—5″   .35—.75

15. *Dentalium longirostrum* Reeve. E.Afr. Translucent shiny amber. Smooth, slim, and long. 2¾″—4″.   3″   1.00

16. *Cancellaria undulata* Sow. N.S.W., Aust. to Tasmania. Cream, with heavy ribs on crossed lines.   1¾″   .50

17. *Turbo speciosus* A. Adams. Great Barrier Reef, Aust. White, with cross mottling of brown and sharp ribs of green.   1¾″   1.00

18. *Cantharidus eximius* Perry. Aust. Olive, with light lines. Glossy and smooth. Largest of Australian Kelp Shells.   1″   .75

19. *Turbo undulatus* Chem. Tasmania. Alternating zig-zag waves of green and white.   2″   1.00

20. *Nassarius papillosus* L. Indo-Pac. Papillose Dog Whelk. White, with orange-brown patch. Elegantly decorated with gracefully patterned papules.   1½″   .35

21. *Turbo fluctuosus* Wood, 1828. Mex. to Peru. Syn: *T. tessellatus* Kiener, 1847-48. Variable. Greyish, with orange, olive-green, or brown markings. Spiraling ribs with dark squares. 1½″—3″.   1½″   .25

22. *Calliostoma cunninghami* Griffith & Pidgeon. N.Zealand. Cream. Spiral lines of orange-brown hyphens. Base is white. 1¼″—2¼″.   2″   1.50

23. *Nassarius arcularis* L. Indo-Pac. Little Box Dog Whelk. Olive to white. Strong pleats on spire.   1″   .25

24. *Neritina cornea* L. New Ireland. Brown. Spiral pattern of figured bands.   3/4″   .30

25. *Distorsio anus* L. Indo-Pac. Old Woman. Whorls are twisted and knobbed. Extensive enameled area about opening. 2″—2½″.   2″   .75

26. *Magilus antiquus* Montfort. Indo-Pac. White and paper-thin. Pear-shaped, with flaring aperture. Tube-forming coral-dweller. Prolongs itself into a tube.   1″   3.00

27. *Distorsio decussatus* Val. Guaymas, Mex. White, with touches of brown. Slender. Long anterior canal. Two denticulations near top of aperture. From deep water.   1¾″   1.00

28. *Distorsio perdistortus* Fulton. Japan. White. Upper whorls tilted in different planes. Cross-ribbed.   1¾″   1.25

29. *Distorsio reticulatus* Röd. Japan. Tan. Cross-ribbed. Fold near top of enameled opening. 2″—3″.   2″   1.00

PLATE 32

Plate 33

1. *Strombus pipus* Röd. Indo-Pac. Syn: *S. papilio* Dill. White, with irregular brown patching. Aperture is purple-brown. Knobby. Fine lines inside outer lip. Not common. 2½" 1.75

2. *Strombus gibberulus* L. Indo-Pac. Humped Strombus. Tan, with spiraling white lines. Upper whorls have swollen varices. Humped penultimate whorl. Purple to occasionally rose band inside outer lip. 2" .25

3. *Strombus labiosus* Wood. E.Afr. to E. Ind. Lipped Strombus. Cream, smoke gray, or yellowish. Spire is ribbed. Columella and flaring outer lip are white. Dredged. 1¾"—2" 1.25

4. *Strombus luhuanus* L. Pac. White, with light brown markings. Purple-brown streak on columella. Inner lip is red-orange. 2" .25

5. *Strombus canarium* L. P.I. Canary Strombus. White and yellow-brown. Smooth thickened outer lip. Pointed spire. 2" .25

6. *Strombus pugilis* L. W.I. Fighting Conch. Cream-orange to salmon-pink. Blue splotch on canal. A color series shows wide variation. Strong shoulder spines, the second row toward spire usually being the larger. Flaring wing and shiny columella. Top end of outer lip is twisted upward. *S. alatus* Gmel., a commoner species, is sometimes offered as *S. pugilis* L. See also No. 9. 3" 1.00

7. *Strombus bulla* Röd. Ryukyu Is. Bubble Strombus. Smooth exterior. Whitish, tan, or purplish. Inside opening is red-orange. Sometimes lavender shading at tip of canal. Spire may be glazed over. 2"—3". 2½" 1.25

8. *Strombus aurisdianae* L. Indo-Pac. Diana's Ear. Rough exterior. Knobs on dorsal side of body whorl. Brown to red-orange aperture. Upper lip is produced, with adjacent fine lines. Siphonal canal is strongly recurved. 2"—3". 2¼" .50

9. *Strombus alatus* Gmel. Fla. to W.I. Wing Strombus. Not to be confused with *S. pugilis* L. The former species has short shoulder spines, and top of wing is not produced. See also No. 6. 3" .50

10. *Strombus epidromis* L. Indo-Pac. Sail Strombus. White, with light brown marking and characteristic flaring lip. Upper part of outer lip reaches to first suture. 3" 1.00

11. *Strombus plicatus columba* Lam. E.Afr. White, with light brown bands. Purple-brown patch on upper part of columella. Irregular blotch on inside of outer lip. 1½" .75

12. *Strombus sinuatus* Humphrey, 1786. P.I. & Pac. Syn: *S. laciniatus* Dill. Brown mottling on white. Purplish pink in aperture. Three or four tongue-like blades at top of outer lip. 3½" 1.50

13. *Strombus raninus* Gmel. Fla. & W.I. Hawk Wing. Grey, with dark brown marking. Pinkish outer lip points upward higher than spire. 2"—4". 2¾" .50

14. *Strombus vittatus campbelli* Griffith & Pidgeon. W.Aust. Syn: *S. campbelli* Gray. Cream, with brown mottlings. Whorls of spire have axial ribs tipped with beads. Faint lines on top and bottom of outer lip. 2¼" 1.00

15. *Strombus aurisdianae aratrum* Röd, 1798. Queensland, Aust. Syn: *Strombus melanostomus* Sow. A variety with dark to black staining about lip. Orange-brown in aperture. 2"—3". 2¼" 1.75

16. *Strombus lentiginosus* L. Indo-Pac. Silver Lip. Whitishgrey spots. Knobbed. Light orange in opening and silvery glaze on columella. 3" .50

17. *Strombus gracilior* Sow. W.Mex. Yellowish brown, with lighter central band. High spire with blunt spines. Orange on edge of lip. 2½"—3". 2¾" .50

18. *Strombus granulatus* Swain. W.Mex. A graceful shell. White, with brown patches. Crinkled and knobbed. Granulations inside outer lip. 2½"—3½" .50—1.00

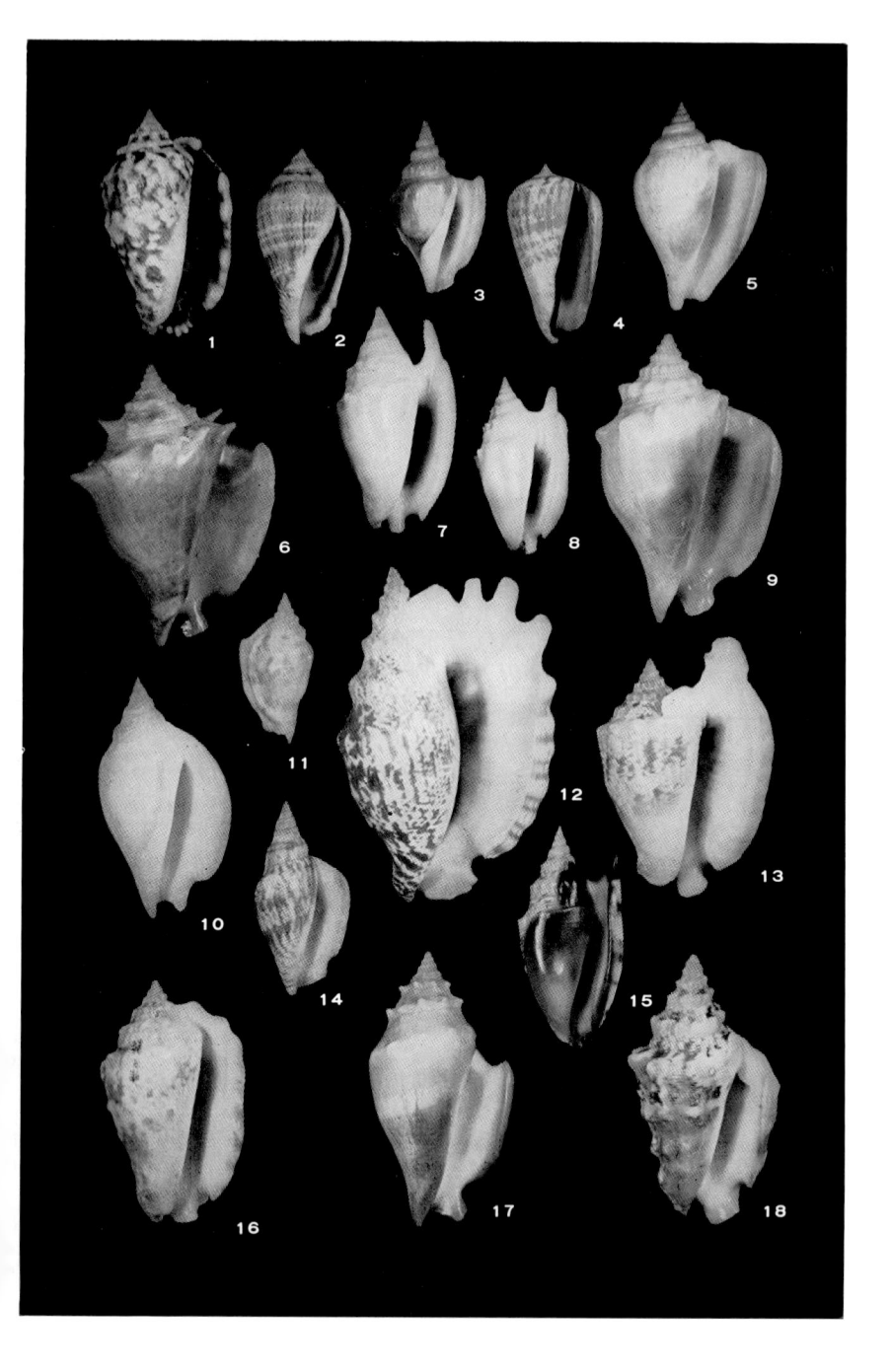

PLATE 33

Plate 34

1. *Cassis (Semicassis) persimilis* Kira. Japan. White to pale flesh color. Faint yellow marks and spiraling cords.
$1\frac{1}{2}''$ .25

2. *Cassis (Semicassis) pila* Reeve. P.I. Smooth white. Bands of brown squares. Lower columella is corded. $1\frac{1}{2}''$ .50

3. *Cassis (Tylocassis) sulcosa* Bruguière. Med. Sea. White, with nodules about shoulders of whorls. Body whorl is reticulated. Lower columella is granulose. Very variable. $1\frac{3}{4}''$ .75

4. *Cassis (Tylocassis) saburon* Adanson. Med. Sea. White. Corded on whorls and columella. $1\frac{1}{4}''$—$2''$. $1\frac{3}{4}''$ 1.00

5. *Cassis (Levenia) coarctata* Sow. La Paz to Ecuador. Pale beige, with vertical streaks of dark brown and rings of nodules dotted with brown. Smaller than *C. tenuis* Wood. $1\frac{3}{4}''$—$2''$. $1\frac{3}{4}''$ 2.50

6. *Cassis chinense* Dillwyn. China. Vertical, wavy, brownish streaks. Descending cords. Brown spots on lip and varix. Long teeth on inner lip. $1\frac{3}{4}''$ 2.00

7. *Cassis (Semicassis) semigranosa* Lam. Tasmania. Cream, and stained brown. Granules high up on body whorl.
$2''$ 1.00

8. *Cassis (Xenogalea) paucirugis* Menke. W.Aust. Shiny ivory, with traces of yellow bands. Faint shoulder nodules. Columella is smooth. $2''$ .75

9. *Cassis (Semicassis) areola* L. Pac. Checkerboard Helmet. Bands of dark brown squares. $2''$—$3''$ .75—1.50

10. *Cassis (Semicassis) japonica* Reeve. Japan. Corded. Bands of pale brown squares. $2''$ .50

11. *Cassis (Xenophalium) collactea* Finlay. N.Zealand. Brownish. Bands of white squares. Nodules on last half of shoulder. Uncommon. $2\frac{1}{4}''$ 1.50

12. *Cassis (Phalium) bandata* Perry. Queensland, Aust. Shiny white, with fulvous bands crossed by paler ones. Sharp triangular nodules on shoulder and spire.
$3''$ 1.50

13. *Cassis (Semicassis) centriquadrata* Val. W.Mex. to Ecuador. Bands of brownish squares. Corded. Granular inner lip.
$2''$ .75

14. *Cassis (Galeodea) echinophora* L. Med. Sea. Prickly Helmet. Brown, with bands of nodules. $2\frac{1}{2}''$ 1.00

15. *Cassis (Cypraecassis) testiculus* L. N.C. to W.I. Baby Bonnet. Light brown, with dark descending waves. Vertical cords. $1''$—$3''$. $2\frac{1}{2}''$ 1.25

16. *Cassis (Phalium) granulata* Born. Fla. to W.I. Scotch Bonnet. Cream, with about 20 spiral cords. Bandings of pale brown patches. Lower columella is granular.
$2''$ .75

17. *Cassis (Xenogalea) pyrum* Lam. N. Zealand. Globular. Cream, with bands of flamelike brown patches. $2''$—$3''$.
$2\frac{1}{2}''$ 1.00

18. *Cassis undulata* Gmel. Sicily. Cream, with waving brown vertical markings. Broad raised bands. Lower inner lip is granular. $3\frac{1}{2}''$ 2.50

19. *Cassis (Phalium) glauca* L. Indo-Pac. Blue-Grey Helmet. Greyish. Orange-brown on columella and lip. Points at anterior end. $3''$—$4''$. $3\frac{1}{2}''$ 1.50

20. *Cassis (Phalium) strigata* Gmel. Japan & Pac. Striped Helmet. Descending brown stripes. $1\frac{3}{4}''$—$4''$. $2\frac{1}{2}''$ .75

21. *Cassis (Hypocassis) bicarinata* Jonas S.Aust. Brownish, with circling hyphens. Two rows of nodules on upper part of body whorl. $3\frac{1}{4}''$ 2.50

22. *Cassis (Cypraecassis) tenuis* Wood. La Paz to Ecuador. Brownish. Ringed with nodules. Panel and lip banded with salmon. Resembles *Cassis rufa* L. Fairly rare.
$2\frac{1}{2}''$ 8.00

23. *Cassis (Phalium) cicatricosa* Gmel. Caribbean. Smooth Scotch Bonnet. Like *Cassis granulata* Born, see No. 16, but with spiral cords smoothed out. $1\frac{1}{2}''$—$2\frac{1}{2}''$.
$1\frac{1}{2}''$ .75

PLATE 34

Plate 35

1. *Bursa californica* Hinds. Calif. to Guaymas. A handsome *Bursa.* Yellow-brown on white, with brown bands. Prominent nodes or horns at shoulders of whorls. 3″—6″.
3″ 1.25

2. *Bursa rana* L. Pac. Somewhat flattened. Pointed horns on shoulders of whorls and on varices. Brown patches, shading to yellow or white. 3″ .75

3. *Bursa foliata* Brod. E.Afr. Most colorful of the genus. Flesh-colored, with bright orange about the toothed aperture.
3″ 1.50

4. *Conus monile* Hwass. Indo-Pac. Cream, circled with brown dots arranged in bands. High spire. 2¼″ 3.75

5. *Conus iodostoma* Reeve. Mozambique. Cream, with orange-brown bands of dots and irregular spots. Spire is pointed.
1⅛″ 5.00

6. *Fasciolaria gigantea* Kiener. Gulf of Mex. Horse Conch. One of the largest of the univalves, adults reaching 1′ long, or occasionally 2′. Rough. Whitish to chalky salmon, with flaking periostracum. Interesting, but beauty is in form rather than in surface texture. Small specimens, like that shown, are bright orange-red and of attractive appearance.
3″ .50, 10″ 5.00, 15″ 8.00 and up

7. *Voluta (Lyria) multicostata* Brod., 1827. S.Aust. Syn: *V. mitraeformis* Lam., 1844. Cream, with brown spots tending to bands. Prominent, slightly S-shaped, riblike varices. 1½″ 1.75

8. *Voluta (Lyria) lyraeformis* Swain. Zanzibar, E.Afr. Slender spire is produced.

Strong rounded ribs. Brown, almost salmon, ringed with wide bands of slightly darker color separated by dark lines. Ribs crossed by fine dark lines. 4″ 60.00 and up

9. *Murex elenensis* Dall. Panamic Prov. Helen Murex. Cream, with short spines which are longer on canal. Faint lavender inside. 2″—3″. 2″ .75

10. *Arca (Trisodos) tortuosa* L. China. Twisted Ark. Valves are twisted. Radiating cords from umbones to edge. Rare.
3″ 1.50

11. *Cymatium rubeculum* L. Indo-Pac. A typical Triton. Variable shades of yellow, reddish, and red. Common brown color 1½″ .60

12. *Cymatium (Mayena) australasium* Perry. Aukland, N.Zealand. Brown, crossed by faint threads. Faint nodules on shoulder. Suture is impressed and uneven.
2½″ 1.00

13. *Stellaria solaris* L. P.I. Light brown. Sloping sides. Paper-thin. Fringed by hollow spines. Rare, and if fine, especially so. 2″ 4.00, 3⅛″ Fine 18.00 and up

14. *Bursa rubeta* L. Pac. Robust with warty appearance. Very rought callus on colomella. Orange to red about aperture. 2½″ 4″. 3″ 1.00

15. *Astraea undosa* Wood. S. Calif. Waved Star. Light brown, with sloping sides. Spiraled by waved rows of nodules. Pearly when polished. 2″—6″.
2″ Natural .50
2″ Polished 1.00

PLATE 35

Plate 36

1. *Voluta (Melo) melo* Sol. S.China Seas. Syn: *V. (Melo) indica* Gmel. Beige, usually with bands of brown patches. Small crown and wide flaring aperture. 4″—10″.
7″   5.00

2. *Strombus gigas* L. Fla. & W.I. Great Conch or Pink Roller. The history and natural history of this ponderous, pink-mouthed beauty would fill a book. It attracts attention by its size, shape, and color and has found uses as a doorstop, garden decoration, and home ornament. It is a nimble beach performer. Many shells are marketed with a hole made in the shoulder to facilitate removal of the animal for food.   8″   Fine 3.75

3. *Cassis tuberosa* L. N.C. to Brazil. King Helmet. Triangular when viewed from any direction. Buffs, browns, and beige. Dark on columella. Cameos with black background are cut against the black under-layer. A favorite ornamental shell. 4″—9″.
4″   3.00

4. *Strombus latissimus* L. Cent. to S.Pac. Descending lines of brown on cream. Aperture is white, edged with flesh color. Heavy. Wide wing extends beyond spire. Not common. 4″—7″.   3.00—5.50

5. *Turbo marmoratus* L. Cent. to S.Pac. Mother of Pearl Shell or Green Snail. Greenish to brown, with pearl interior. Bright green and pearl when polished. Heavy and stocky. Scarce because some countries ban export to protect the button industry.   3″—8″ Natural 1.50—5.00
5½″ Polished   7.50

6. *Cassis madagascarensis* Lam. N.C. to W.I. Queen Helmet. Cream, with brown marks. Outer lip and parietal shield are salmon. Heavy. Three spiral rows of large blunt spines. Used for cameos. It does not occur in Madagascar, for which it was inexplicably named. 5″—9″.   5″   4.50

7. *Murex ramosus* Lam. Ind.Oc. White, with superb branching processes, tinted with pink. Pink parietal wall. Along with *M. brassica*, among the largest of the Muricidae. 3″—8″.
Fine 3″ .75, 7″   5.00

8. *Cassis rufa* L. E.Afr. Cameo Shell or Bull Mouth. Distinguished color and form. Body whorl ornamented with rounded chocolate-brown nodules. Shiny finish on wide lip and parietal wall. Inner lip is shiny red with black striations. Sent to Italy years ago, it became the original material for the art of Cameo. 3″—6″.   3″ .75, 6″   3.50

9. *Bursa bubo.* L. Pac. Syn: *B. lampas* Lam. Brown on cream. Granulated and tuberculated whorls. Rough and usually lime coated. Largest of the genus. Specimen shown 9″.   8″   3.50

10. *Cassis cornuta* L. Indo-Pac. Horned Helmet. Whitish. Strong blunt nodules. Wide, shiny outer lip and parietal wall are white to flesh-color. Interior is golden brown. Recently-caught huge specimens seen less often than formerly. Often found in old homes since in the 18th and 19th centuries they were brought in by sailing ships as ballast. To 12″.
7½″ 3.00, 11½″   8.50

11. *Tonna cepa* Röd. S.W.Pac. Syn: *T. olearia* L. A deep brown globe, circled by sculptured bands with lines between. Perhaps largest of the genus. 3″—8″.
4″ 1.00, 7″   5.00

PLATE 36

Plate 37

1. *Murex ternispina* Lam. Indo-Pac. & China Sea to Aust. Triple Spined Murex. Near-white, and sometimes banded. Spines on canal are farther apart than on *Murex triremis* Perry Lam. Has a similar short erect spine on outer lip. 3½"—5".
3½" 1.25

2. *Murex nigritus* Phil. Gulf of Calif. Blackened Murex. A growth series shows that young shells are nearly white, and as they grow they become clouded and then marked with black. This shell has a higher spire and longer canal than *Murex radix* Gmel. Also, it is less chunky, and the shoulder spines are farther apart. Reeve, in his *Concologica Iconica*, distinguished a third species, *Murex ambiguus* Reeve (3" 3.50), which has a light structure and fronds which are large, open, and flowery. To 6".
3" .75, 5½" 3.00

3. *Murex radix* Gmel. Panama to Ecuador. Lumpier than *Murex nigritus* Phil. and blacker looking because close spines touch and even overlap. Also, habitat is more southern. Reeve says, "distinguished by its massive structure, round globose form, and by the numerous varices-compressed, stunted growth of scales." To 6".
2" 1.25, 4½" 4.00

4. *Murex erythrostomus* Swain., 1831. Gulf of Calif. to Peru. Rose Murex. Syn: *Murex bicolor* Val., 1832. Body whorl is white, sometimes trimmed with pink. A favorite because of its flaring pink aperture. Much variation in quality and color.
3" .75, 4¼" 2.00

5. *Murex brandaris* Lam. Italy. Beige or cream, with bright yellow-brown on aperture. Flat sides of whorls produce a neat boxlike effect. The ancients prepared the famed Tyrian purple dye from the secretion of the animal's glands.
2¼" .50

6. *Murex cornutus* Lam. W.Afr. Horned Murex. Brown, with low curved spines. Scarce.
5" 5.00

7. *Murex (Forreria) belcheri* Hinds. Calif. Light brown on white. Perfect adults have a strong point on outer lip just below body whorl.
3" 4.50

8. *Murex fulvescens* Sow. N.C. to E.Mex. Stocky, with strong hollow spines. May be brownish with fine brown lines against white. The better specimens come from deep water and are regarded as semi-rare. Largest species of the genus in the Western Atlantic. To 6".
3½" 2.00, 5" 5.00

9. *Thais patula* L.S. Fla to W.I. Dye Shell. Syn: *Purpura p.* L. Knobby exterior. Flaring aperture, with opening edged with salmon-pink. Small operculum. Exudes a harmless fluid which, on white cloth, turns green and later purple. To 3".
2" .60

10. *Murex regius* Wood. W.Mex. to Peru. Royal Murex. Valued for color. White, with pink aperture. Columellar lip is pink, shading to black. Varices are reflected and doubled. To 5".
3¼" 2.00

11. *Rapana thomasiana* Crosse. Japan. White to brown. Spiraled with dark hyphens. Flattened whorls. Very wide orange-salmon aperture and large operculum.
4½" 1.50

12. *Murex troscheli* Lisch. Giant Venus Comb. A spectacular Spiny Murex. Long sharp spines on crown, body, and canal which are seldom all perfect.
6" With good spines 3.50

PLATE 37

Plate 38

1. *Murex zealandica* Quoy & Gaimard. N. Zealand. Delicate, with long spines. Fine specimens scarce.   1″ 1.00, 2″ 3.00

2. *Murex vespertilio* Kuroda. Japan. Delicate winged species.   1¼″ 2.25

3. *Murex cervicornis* Lam. N.E.Aust. Delicate. Long spines separating into "deer horns."   1¼″ 2.00, 2¼″ 6.00

4. *Murex florifer arenarius* Clench. Lace Murex. Light brown, with profuse fernlike fronds.   2½″ 2.50

5. *Murex clavus* Kien. P.I. & Japan. Key Murex. Syn: *Murex elongatus* Sol., but not *M. elongatus* Lam. Much prized for its astonishing form. White, with wide wing and high spire. Rare.   3″ 30.00 and up

6. *Murex triremis* Perry, 1811. Japan. Venus Comb. Syn: *M. tenuispina* Lam., 1822. The wings of the long curved spines are very subject to breakage. One of those fascinating shells wanted by most collectors. 4″—6″.   4½″ 3.00

7. *Murex anatomicus* Perry. Japan. Fanlike fronds which are large on outer lip and smaller on body whorl. See No. 9.   1½″ 3.00

8. *Murex eurypteron* Adams and Reeve. Broad-Winged Murex. Graceful flaring wings with ends turned back.   2″ 1.00

9. *Murex anatomicus zamboi* Burch & Burch, 1960. Olango Is., Cebu. Variety with long spines having split ends. Named after Evaristo Zambo of Mandawa, Cebu. See No. 7.   2″ 6.00

10. *Latiaxis pagodus* A. Adams. Japan. Syn: *L. spinosus* Hirase. Spire ringed with crown of curved spines.   1″ 2.00

11. *Latiaxis lischkeanus* Dunker. Japan. Translucent white, fringed with feathery fronds or spines.   1½″ 2.75

12. *Latiaxis deburghiae* Reeve. Japan. A simple, small, scarce species with wide aperture and serrations on the spire. Angle of photograph hides the rounding plain body whorl. Rare.   1⅛″ 6.00

13. *Latiaxis mawae* Griffith & Pidgeon. Japan. Pinkish at times and white inside. Spire forms a sloping platform. Its intriguing shape helps to make this a much-wanted species.   1¾″ 5.00

14. *Latiaxis japonicus* Kuroda. Japan. Frills circle the body whorl, and broad serrations circle the high spire.   1½″ 1.00

PLATE 38

Plate 39

1. *Murex nigrospinosus* Reeve. Pac. Black-Tipped Murex. A spiny shell, with tips of spines darkened.   3″ 1.50

2. *Murex haustellum* L. P.I. Snipe Bill. Body forms a swollen knob. Canal is long and often spineless.   4″ 2.00

3. *Murex asianus* Kuroda. Japan. Syn: *M. elongatus* Lam., but not *M. elongatus* Sol. which is synonym for *M. clavus* Kiener. Brown and beautifully frondose, but processes more intact in the smaller specimens.   5″ 3.00

4. *Murex centrifugus* Hinds. W. Mex. Syn: *M. swansoni* Hertlein and Strong. Slightly yellowed white to light brown. Fronds recurved. Deep water.   3″ 3.50

5. *Murex trunculus* L. Med. Sea. Banded Murex. Stocky, with dark bands.
2½″ .60

6. *Conus prometheus* Hwass. W.Afr. Cream background. A graceful shell, with elevated spire and rounded crown which is mottled cream and tan. Body is circled with dots and hyphens of orange-tan, forming bands of darker color. To 8″.   4½″ 5.00

7. *Conus amadis* Gmel. Ceylon. Coffee brown, with rows of sidewise tents that thin out to leave two dark bands. Crown is high, and spire is pointed.   2½″ 3.75

8. *Murex pliciferoides* Kuroda. Japan. Pleated Murex. White, tinged with brown. A popular shell with typical characteristics of the *Muricidae* in spire, body, and spines.
3¾″ .75

9. *Murex permaestus* Hedley P.I. Sad Murex. Syn: *M. capucinus* L. Rounded, with no spines. Almost black, but light aperture.   2″ 1.00

10. *Murex triformis* Reeve. S.Aust. Brown, with winged varices. Seldom found with processes well developed. Scarce.
2″ 1.50

11. *Murex pomum* Gmel. W.Atlan.Oc. Apple Murex. Sturdy shell, with dark blotches on outer lip and above aperture. 2″—4½″.   2¾″ .75

12. *Murex endivia* Lam. P.I. Endive Murex. Handsome, with alternate black and white bands. Some specimens poorly developed, and others richly frondose.
2½″ .60, 3¼″ 2.00

13. *Murex brassica* Lam. W. Mex. Cabbage Murex. Chunky. White, with three brown bands. Edges of flat varices are embroidered in rose, and columella is rose. Fine large deep-water specimens of striking appearance and of fine color are scarce.
3″ 1.00, 6″ 5.00

PLATE 39

Plate 40

1. *Cassis (Xenogalea) achatina* Lam. S. Afr. Tan, with brown and white marks in circular bands. Aperture has white callus over inner lip. This type has a smooth shoulder. See also No. 2. 2″ .75

2. *Cassis (Xenogalea) achatina* Lam. S. Afr. Same species as No. 1. This type has two rows of knobs at shoulder. 2⅛″ 1.25

3. *Lotorium cutaceum* L. S.Afr. Brown, with white opening. Upper whorls are crownlike. Conspicuous cuticle on fresh specimens. 2¼″ .75

4. *Cardium (Lophocardium) annettae* Dall. Baja Calif. to Costa Rica. Orange to cerise. Fragile. Open at end. Concentric ribs. Rare. 1½″ 2.00

5. *Buccinum lagenaria* Lam. S.Afr. Syn: *Cominella l.* Lam. Brownish, with brown and white bands. 1½″ .75

6. *Turritella carinifera* Lam. S.Afr. Rough. Brown to white, with raised keel circling at periphery of each whorl. 3″ .75

7. *Cypraea angustata* Gmel. S.Afr. Fuscous-Toothed Cowry. Syn: *C. fuscodentata* Gray. Brown mottling on beige. Beige base entirely crossed by heavy yellow-brown teeth. Good beach specimen. 1″ 1.00

8. *Murex oxycantha* Brod. Panamic Prov. Cream, with brown spines in vertical rows and edging aperture. About eight varices, crossed by scaly ribs. Not common. 2″ 6.00

9. *Lotorium klenei* Sow. S.Afr. Beige. Highly knobbed, fine, cream ridges circling whorls. Prominent spire and deep sutures. 1½″ .65

10. *Turritella sanguinea* Reeve. S.Afr. Cream, with many interrupted circling bands. Each whorl is rounded at suture. 2″—3″. 3″ .75

11. *Haliotis spadicea* Donovan. S.Afr. Syn: *H. sanguinea* Hanley. Peach-red on back, if not eroded. Slightly reddish interior. Wrinkled, with many openings. 2½″ 1.00

12. *Bullia laevissima* Gmel. S.Afr. Plough Shell. Beige, with large columella callus. Brown band encircling spire. 1⅜″ 1.00

13. *Lotorium africanum* A. Adams. S.Afr. Brown, with snowy white aperture. Tends to have cream bands. Finely reticulated, vertically and horizontally. 3″ 1.25

14. *Cymatium gibbosum adairense* Dall. W.Mex. Angular knobs. Narrow at sutures, producing spiral staircase effect. 1⅜″ 2.25

15. *Argobuccinum argus* Gmel. S.Afr. Tan, with brown and cream bands circling shell. Fine brown lines between bands. Broadest near top of shoulder. White aperture. 1¾″—4″. 2″ 2.00

16. *Fasciolaria heynemanni* Dunker. S.Afr. Dark brown, with white aperture. Small knobs at shoulder. White nucleus similar to that of *Volutidae*. 2″ 1.50

PLATE 40

Plate 41

1. *Ficus gracilis* Sow. China. Spiraling brown cords and vertical brown lines cross to form a network. See also Plate 47, No. 19.
5″   2.50

2. *Ficus subintermedius* d'Orbigny. Japan. Brownish, with narrow lighter bands with dark brown patches.   3″   .50

3. *Ficus papyratia* Say. N.C. to Gulf Mex. Paper Fig. Thin, whitish spiraling cords crossing finer descending cords. 3″—4″.
3½″   .50

4. *Ficus ventricosa* Sow., 1825. W.Mex. Syn: *Ficus decussata* Wood, 1828. Brownish, with brown spots on strong spiral ridges. Aperture is lavender. 3½″—4″.
3½″   .60

5. *Latirus polygonus* Gmel. Mozambique. Yellow-brown. Spiral cords with nodules. Black patches on vertical ridges.
2¼″   1.00

6. *Melongena pugilina* Born. Ind.Oc. Rich brown, with spiny notches at shoulder. 3″—4″.   3″   .50

7. *Thais armigera* Link. Stocky. Armed with thick rounded nodules. Aperture is yellow to pink. Dull finish.   2½″   1.00

8. *Colus stimpsoni* Mörch. Labrador to Me. Stimpson's Whelk. White, with rough textured surface and recurved canal. Green-brown periostracum. Deep water. 3″—3½″.
3″   .75

9. *Latirus smaragdula* L. Indo-Pac. Globose. Adjacent spirals of orange-brown and dark brown.   1¼″   .60

10. *Purpura persica* Lam. P.I. Overall blackish brown. Corded with white dashes.

Pink on columella. 2″—3″.   2½″   1.00

11. *Cerithium vertagus* L. Indo-Pac. White. Crumpling on shoulders of whorls.
1¾″   .25

12. *Melongena corona* Gmel. Fla. Famous Crown Conch. In earlier days often collected by St. Petersburg tourists. White and brown bandings. Spines on crown vary fantastically. There are many slightly differing races. See also No. 16.   4″   1.00

13. *Cerithium obeliscus* Brug. N.Aust. & Fiji to Hawaii. Cream, black hieroglyphics and sharp points on shoulder bands of whorls. Aperture side is flattened. Facets glisten. 1½″—2¼″.   1½″   .25

14. *Purpura patula pansa* Gould. W.Mex. Grey, with dark nodules. Flat orange-brown columella with white inner margin. Often confused with East Coast *P. patula* L., which has no white on columella. 1½″—3½″.
1½″   .50

15. *Melongena melongena* L. W.I. & Campeche, Mex. Brown Crown Conch. Brown, with yellowish and white bands. Usually has sharp spines on shoulder and body whorl. 2½″—4″.   2½″   1.00

16. *Melongena corona* Gmel. Fla. This is a specimen of a small race, with its own type of banding, crown, and spines, contrasting with No. 12.   3¼″   1.50

17. *Melongena patula* Brod. & Sow. W. Mex. to Panama. Chocolate brown. Banded with coffee brown to white. Usually with sharp spines on shoulder. Pink on smooth columella and inside. To 10″.
4¼″   1.00

PLATE 41

Plate 42

1. *Voluta (Aulica) flavicans* Gmel. Aust. Syns: *V. tissotiana* Crosse, *V. quaesita* Ired., *V. signifer* Brod., and *V. kellneri* Ired. Solid and stocky. Some have squarish nodules around shoulder. White to cream, with faint wavy bandings of brown to blue-grey. Four plaits on columella. Most variable. See Plate 26, No. 26. This type 12.00
2½" Without nodules 6.00 and up

2. *Voluta (Amoria) zebra* Leach. East Aust. Cream, with deep, sharply defined, descending brown lines which occasionally meet.
1½" 1.25

3. *Voluta (Amoria) zebra* Leach. East Aust. Pinkish brown, with fine descending red-brown lines. Another species, *Voluta (Amoria) lineata* Leach, is like No. 2, but with more separated longitudinal lines which do not usually meet. 1½" 1.00

4. *Cassis (Morum) tuberculosa* Sow. Panamic Prov. Cone-shaped. White, with black markings and rings of flattened black tubercles. White callus and aperture. Teeth on inner lip. Scarce. 1¼" 1.25

5. *Delphinula imperialis* Lam. P.I. Shoulder and crown have long spine curving toward spire. Round pearly aperture. 2" 7.50

6. *Murex monodon* Sow. N.W.Aust. Syn: *M. cornucervi* Bolten. Brown, with dark curling spines. Pink columella and a prominent point or tooth just below middle of outer lip. Specimens vary much in color and curling of spines. In fine specimens, one of the anterior spines loops back over the body whorl. Fine specimens scarce.
4" 10.00 and up

7. *Vasum ceramicum* L. P.I. Pottery Vase. Stocky and rough. White under dark circling bands. Heavy spurs on body whorl and spire. Columella with three plaits with sub-plaits between. Not common.
4½" 3.75

8. *Harpa costata* L. Mauritius. Syn: *H. imperialis* Lam. Looks somewhat like *Harpa major* Röd. in shape and color, but has many ribs. Wide aperture which, with columella, may be stained with bright yellow. Callus, perhaps yellowed, extends to form a ridge around the spire. Spire shows excessively fine ribbing. Specimen shown here has 34 ribs. There is a noticeable notch where, after the inner lip meets the lower columella, the edge of the whorl is heavily pleated. Rare. 2"—3".
3" 40.00 and up

9. *Cantharus gemmatus* Reeve. Panamic Prov. Brown and white. Raised black lines ring the periphery of the body. Plait near top of opening. 1½" .75

10. *Cancellaria cassidiformis* Sow. Panamic Prov. Flesh color to orange, with whitish band on lower part of body whorl. Shiny callus on columella. See also Plate 26 No. 29. 1½" 1.25

11. *Mitra taeniata* Lam. N.E.Aust. Syn: *Mitra vittata* Swain. Banding in series of orange, black, and white. Swollen ribs descending on spire and body whorl.
2½" 10.00

Plate 43

1. *Trophonopsis candelabrum* Reeve. Japan. Neat, squarish sculpture. 1⅜" 2.25

2. *Pyramidella gigantea* Dunker. Japan. White. Spiraling threads. 1¼" .50

3. *Cymatium loebbeckei* Lisch. Japan.
1¼" .50

4. *Bullina nobilis* Habe. Japan. Lovely rose pattern on white. Rare. ¾" 5.00

5. *Mitra (Scabricola) papilio* Link. P.I.
1¼" .85

6. *Latirus turritus* Gmel. P.I. Brown lines on cream. 1⅛" .50

PLATE 42

Plate 43 (cont.)

7. *Mitra (Pterygia) undulosa* Reeve. E.Afr. Vertical waving and brown banding. See also No. 13. $1\frac{1}{4}''$ 1.00

8. *Mitra ambigua* Swain. Japan. Brown, with white banding. $1\frac{1}{2}''$ .50

9. *Mitra (Strigatella) amphorella* Lam. Japan. Dark brown. $1\frac{1}{2}''$ .50

10. *Mitra intermedia* Kiener. E.Afr. White bands on purple-brown. Incorrectly identified in some books.
     $1\frac{3}{4}''$ .60, $2\frac{1}{4}''$ .90

11. *Mitra puncticulata* Lam. P.I. Turreted. Orange bands. $2''$ 1.50

12. *Mitra rugosa* Gmel. P.I. Syn: *M. corrugata* Lam. Black bands vertical ribs.
     $1\frac{1}{2}''$ .60

13. *Mitra (Pterygia) undulosa* Reeve. E. Afr. Vertical waving. See also No. 7.
     $1\frac{1}{4}''$ 1.00

14. *Mitra (Strigatella) scutulata* Gmel. Japan. Dark brown, with cream patches.
     $1\frac{1}{4}''$ .65

15. *Mitra (Cancilla) praestantissima* Röd. Japan. Red-brown spirals. $1\frac{1}{4}''$ 2.00

16. *Mitra exasperata* Gmel. Japan. Vertical ribs. $\frac{3}{4}''$ .50

17. *Mitra regina* Sow. E.Afr. Lovely variable banding of red, orange, or yellow. Rare. $2\frac{1}{2}''$ 8.00

18. *Mitra granatina* Lam. Japan. White, with band of interrupted brown lines.
     $2''$ 1.50

19. *Mitra (Imbricaria) conica* Schum. E. Ind. & Pac. Looks like a grey cone.
     $1\frac{1}{8}''$ .60

20. *Mitra (Scabricola) hirasei* Pilsbry. Japan. Faint pinkish bands. $1\frac{1}{8}''$ .60

21. *Cassidula auris-felis* Brug. China to Singapore. Cat's Ear. Brown. From brackish water. $1''$ .75

22. *Cassidula angulifera* Petit. New Caledonia to Queensland, Aust. Brown. Angular shoulder. From brackish water.
     $1''$ .50

23. *Conus cinereus* Hwass. P.I. Syn: *C. stramineus* Lam. Grey, with bands of brown squares. $1\frac{1}{2}''$ 2.50

24. *Turbo coronatus* Gmel. Like a woven basket. $\frac{3}{4}''$ .40

25. *Turris jeffreysi* Smith. Japan. Brown. Turreted. $2''$ .75

26. *Cancellaria reticulata* L. Fla. Brown banding on white. $1\frac{3}{8}''$ .35

27. *Chiton (Katherina) tunicata* Wood. Aleutians to S.Calif. Black Katy. Shown without girdle. $2''-3''$. $2\frac{1}{2}''$ 1.00

28. *Chiton (Tonicella) lineata* Wood. Aleutians to Santiago. Brown pattern of triangles and lines with girdle. $\frac{3}{4}''-1\frac{1}{2}''$.
     $1\frac{1}{4}''$ 1.00

29. *Conus piperatus* Dillwyn. N.E.Aust. Syn: *C. imperator* Woolacott.Grey-brown. with light band. Coronated. $1\frac{1}{4}''$ 1.00

30. *Purpura clavigera* Küster. Japan. Black knobs on white. $1\frac{1}{2}''$ .50

31. *Conus praecellens* A. Adams. Japan. Brown bands and dots on white. See also Plate 49, No. 7. $1\frac{1}{4}''$ 2.00

32. *Nassarius obsoletus* Say. Gulf of St. Lawr. to Fla. and introduced to Pac. Coast. Black Dog Whelk. Spire is eroded.
     $\frac{7}{8}''$ 5 for .25

33. *Nassarius reticulatus* Lam. Italy. Whitish. Waved ribs on brown.
     $\frac{7}{8}''$ .25

34. *Murex axicornis* Lam. E.Aust. Long dark fronds on light brown.
     $1\frac{1}{4}''-2\frac{1}{2}''$ 2.00—5.00

35. *Haliotis ovina* Gmel. West Pac. Syn: *H. latilabris* Phil. Colorful, pearl inside. See also Plate 46, No. 33. $2\frac{1}{2}''$ .75

36. *Cassis (Nannocassis) nana* Tenison Woods. E.Aust. Nodulose Helmet. Triangular. $1\frac{1}{2}''$ 2.00

37. *Amphibola crenata* Mart. Aukland. N. Zealand. Brown. $\frac{7}{8}''$ .40

38. *Babylonia papillaris* Sow. Natal, S.Afr. Syn: *Eburna papillaris* Sow. Ivory. Neat sculpture. Brown mottling. $1\frac{3}{4}''$ 1.00

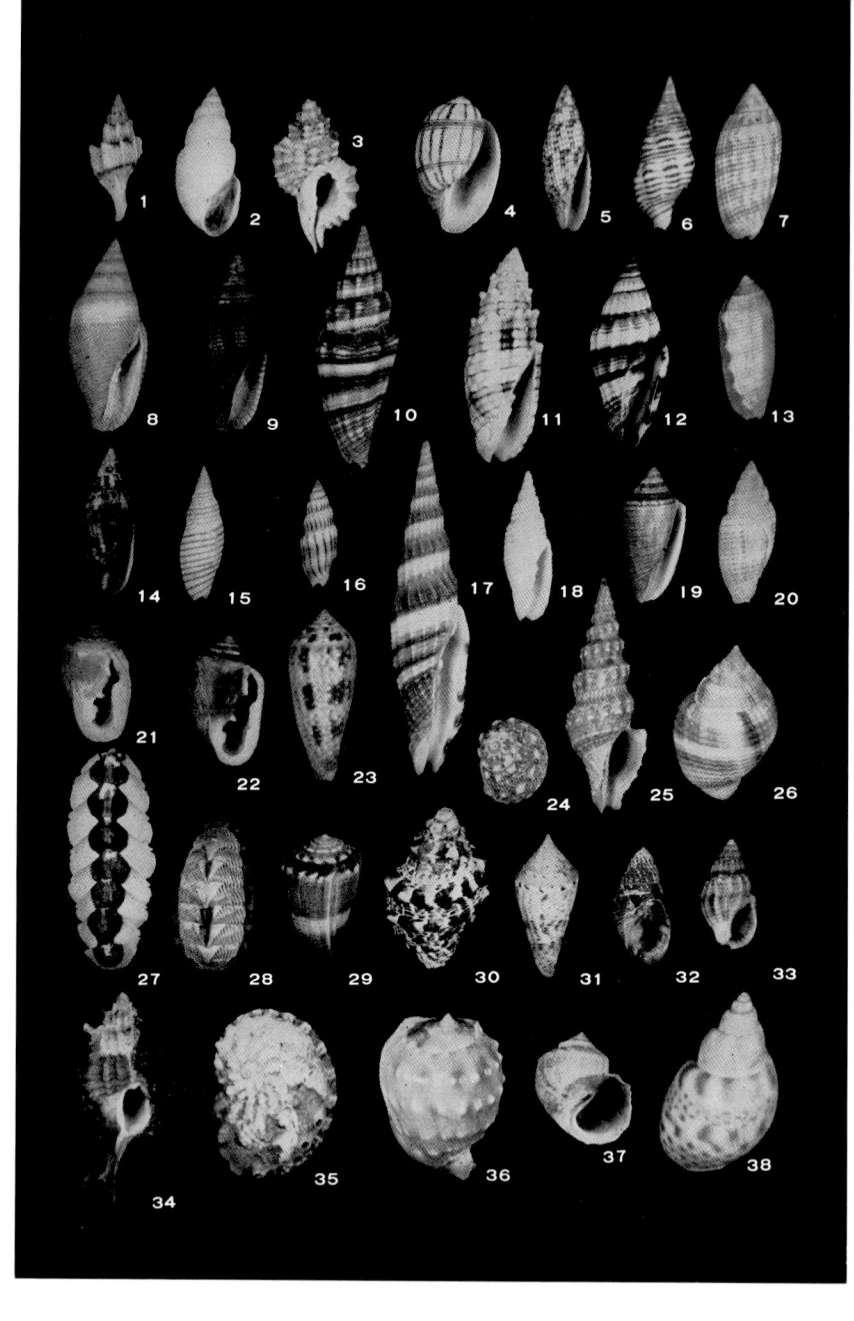

PLATE 43

Plate 44

1. *Buccinum (Neptunea) fukueae* Kira. Japan. Light coffee-brown to cream.
3″ 1.25

2. *Conus iodostoma* Reeve. Mozambique. Orange-tan banding and dotting on white. Rare. See also Plate 35, No. 5.
1⅛″ 5.00

3. *Voluta (Teremachia) tibiaeformis* Kuroda. Japan. Brown, shaded to dark brown. Graceful swollen whorls. Slender high spire. Fluted on upper whorls. Rare.
3″ 12.00

4. *Cypraea ocellata* L. Ceylon. Brown, covered with dots, a few black ones forming "eyes." Lower sides dotted with brown. Strong teeth.
¾″ 1.00

5. *Struthiolaria papulosa* Mart. N.Zealand. Brown vertical streaks. Shoulder and spire ridged with nodules.
2½″ 1.00

6. *Cypraea inocellata differens* Schilder. Japan. Pale brown, with many round white dots. Lower sides and base are white. Very strong teeth. Deep water. Form of *C. miliaris* Gmel.
1½″ 1.00

7. *Murex acanthodes* Watson. N.E.Aust. Cream. Two intervarical ribs. Spiral threads different from *M. macgillivrayi* Dohrn.
2¾″ 3.00

8. *Buccinum pamphagus* Dall. Wash. Pure white. Gracefully swollen whorls circled by spiraling white threads. Found in deep water.
1½″ .60

9. *Conus profundorum* Kuroda. Japan. Broad brown band at top of body whorl. Lower down, lighter banding on cream. High sloping spire. Deep water cone.
2¾″ 15.00

10. *Conus teremachii* Kuroda. Japan. White to flesh color. Slender high spire. Concave between spiraling ridges which have characteristic knobbing and crenulation. Rough surface, but distinguished form. Small operculum with some serration. Rare.
3⅝″ 28.00

11. *Argonauta hians* Sol. P.I. May be dark brown to white. Wrinkled sides edged by nodules. 2″—3½″.
2½″ 3.00

12. *Struthiolaria vermis* Mart. N.Zealand. Pale brown to white. Straight-sided whorls and faint nodules. Smooth lip and columella.
1½″ .60

13. *Aporrhais pes-pelicani* L. Med.Sea. Syn: *Chenopus pes-pelicani* L. Novel shape, making it easy to imagine it looks like a pelican's foot.
1½″ .65

14. *Cymatium wiegmanni* Anton. S.Calif. to Peru. Syn: *Triton chemnitzii* Reeve. Yellow-brown. Spirals vertically crossed by raised ridges. Low nodules on shoulders of whorls.
3″ 1.50

15. *Architectonica nobilis* Röd. Fla. Syn: *A. granulata* Lam. Cream. Spiraling brown granulations and dots. As in other shells of this genus, the umbilicus is open to the spire.
1″ .75

16. *Aporrhais occidentalis mainensis* C.W. Johnson. N.S. to Mt. Desert. Duck's Foot. From a few to 200 fms. Seldom on beaches, but sometimes from fishermen's nets. This variety of *occidentalis* has 14 axial ribs instead of the 22-25 in typical form. Scarce.
1½″ 5.00

PLATE 44

Plate 45

1. *Conus sieboldi* Reeve. Japan. Fine slender form with irregular brown mottling. See also No. 5 and Plate 54, No. 25. 2¼"—3¾". 2¾" 1.00

2. *Conus aculeiformis* Reeve. E.Afr. Needle Cone. White and elongated. Delicate brown mottling in bands. 1½" 3.50

3. *Conus fergusoni* Sow. W.Mex. Stocky and rough. All white, but young cones may have faint yellowish bands. Scarce. 2"—5½". 2½" 2.00, 5½" 7.00

4. *Conus cancellatus* Hwass. Japan. White, with high spire and brownish banding. 1½" .75

5. *Conus sieboldi* Reeve. Japan. Scarce all-white specimen. See also No. 1 and Plate 54, No. 25. 2¾" 1.75

6. *Conus aristophanes* Sow. Indo-Pac. Coronated, with spiraling nodules and brown mottling. Like the less granular *C. coronatus* Gmel. of which it is a sub-species. 1" .50

7. *Conus aurora* Lam. S. Afr. (Classified as *C. caffer-secutor* Crosse according to Turton in his *Marine Shells of Port Alfred*.) Deep brown, and lavender within. Good beach specimens. 1¾" 1.00

8. *Conus caledonicus* Hwass. New Caledonia. Syn: *C. suffusus* Sow. Pinkish. 2" 16.00

9. *Conus tinianus* Hwass. S.Afr. (According to Turton, as in No. 7.) Alternate bands of light mottling and brown. Good beach specimens. 1¾" 1.00

10. *Conus chaldeus* Röd. Indo-Pac. Syn: *C. vermiculatus* Lam. Black-brown on white. Nodules on shoulder. Raised vertical ribs. ⅝" .50

11. *Conus eburneus* Hwass. Indo-Pac.White, circled by squarish black dots. Sometimes faint yellow bands. 1"—2". 2" 1.00

12. *Conus eburneus polyglottus* Weinkauff. P.I. Close bands of wide, black, hyphen-shaped dots. Light brownish bands on white. 1¾" 1.75

13. *Conus virgo* L. P.I. Smooth. Yellow, tipped with purplish. 2"—4½". 3¼" 1.50

14. *Conus pulicarius* Hwass. P.I. Flea-Bitten Cone. Bands of black dots on white. 1¾" .80

15. *Conus glaucus* L. Quezon, P.I. Grey with rings of fine hyphens. 1½" 2.00

16. *Conus arenatus* Hwass. Indo-Pac. Dotted Cone. White, with bandings in waves of tiny dark dots. 1"—2". 1⅝" .50

17. *Conus magus* L. Indo-Pac. Syn: *C. raphanus* Hwass. Very variable in form and coloration so that there are many variety names. 1¾" .50

18. *Conus maldivus* Hwass. E.Afr. Color and pattern vary. 1½"—3". 2" 1.75

19. *Conus brunneus* Wood. The Brown Cone. Dark brown, with white blotches. Yellowish on anterior canal. 1⅜"—2½". 1½" 2.50

20. *Conus lividus* Hwass. Indo-Pac. Yellowish olive, with lighter bands. Purplish aperture. Like *C. flavidus* Lam., but *C. lividus* has coronated spire. 1½" .50

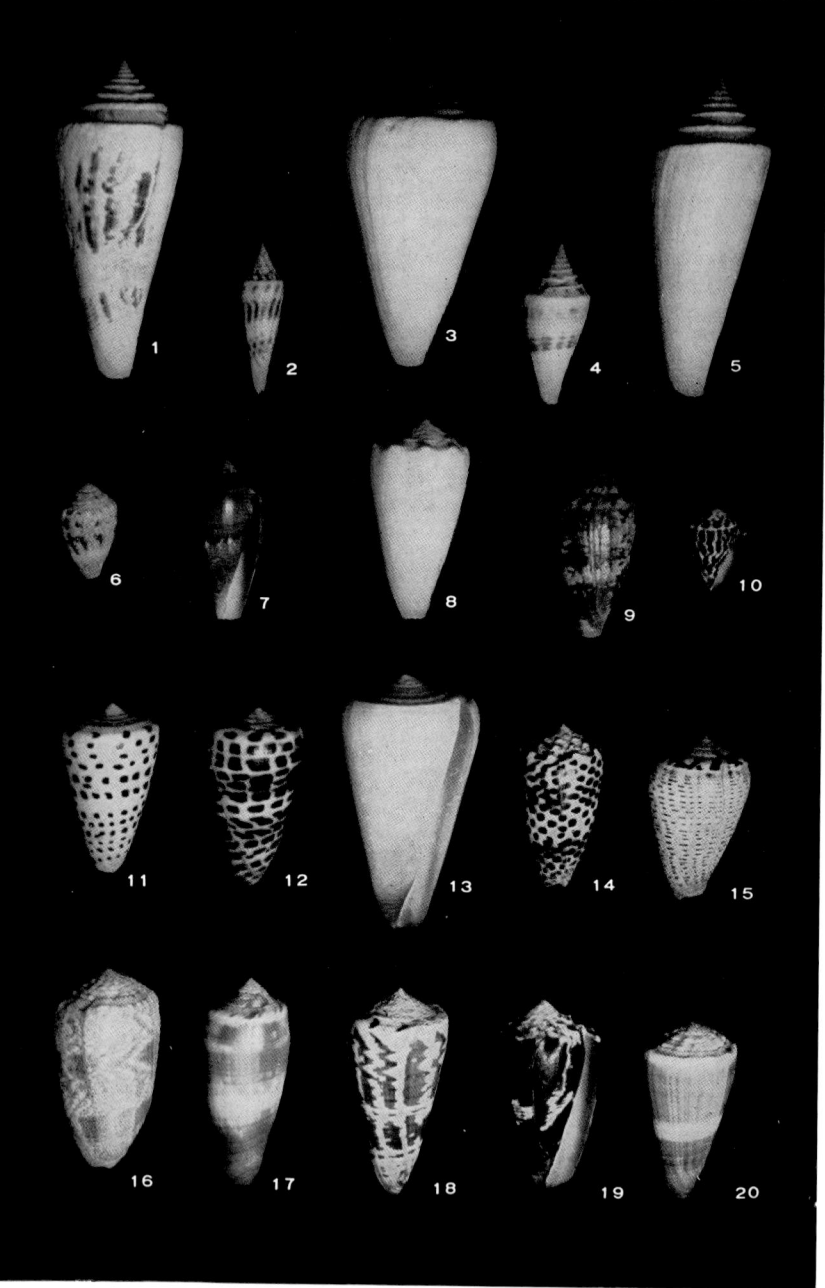

PLATE 45

Plate 46

1. *Conus clarki* Rehder and Abbott. Tex. & La. Syn: *C. frisbeyae* Clench and Pulley. Cord of beads forming brown dots. 1¼″ 15.00 and up

2. *Latiaxis eugeniae* Bernardi. Japan. Plump, with circling lines. 1⅜″ 6.00

3. *Conus sennottorum* Rehder & Abbott. Tortugas to Yucatan. White, with pale brown dots. 1″—1½″. 1¼″ 6.00 and up

4. *Cymatium (Biplex) microstomum* Fulton. Japan. Flat and shiny. 1½″ 1.25

5. *Isocardia vulgaris* Reeve. P.I. Unusual triangular scrolls at top. Scarce. 1¼″ 2.00

6. Same as No. 5

7. *Chiton (Chaetopleura) apiculata* Say. Cape Cod to Fla. Rows of beads. Buff in the north, but colors in Florida. ⅓″—¾″. ½″ .50

8. *Cymatium (Biplex) hirasei* Kuroda & Habe. Recently named. Flattened and brownish. Ribs and varices cross. 1³⁄₁₆″ 2.00

9. *Busycon coarctatum* Sow. 25 fms. off Campeche, E.Mex. Turnip-shaped. Dark spines on shoulder. Long fragile canal. For 100 years supposed to be extinct, but dredged by shrimp boats about 1950. Scarce. 3¾″ 5.00

10. *Mitra Isabella* Swainson. Japan. Corded. Descending orange-brown staining. 2½″ 2.50

11. *Syrinx aruanus* L. Aust. Syn: *Megalatractus proboscidifera* Lam. This grows to be what is probably the largest shell in the world. Here is shown the nucleus from which it begins attached to a tiny specimen. Large specimens lose the nucleus. See Plate 53, No. 11. This form 1½″ .50

12. *Epitonium (Amaea) mitchelli* Dall Tex. to Yucatan. Dark brown band on whorls. About 22 ribs per whorl. Rare. 1¼″—2″. 1½″ 20.00, higher price with operculum

13. *Latirus infundibulum* Gmel. W.I. Spindle-shape and swollen. Vertical ribs and brown circling lines. 2½″ 5.00

14. *Tibia fusus* L. P.I. One of the world's most spectacular shells. Rare because fragile and scarce. Other species with shorter canals are *T. curta* Reeve., *T. recurvirostris* Lam., and *T. powisi* Petit. Adults of *T. fusus* 7″ 15.00 and up

15. *Murex cailleti* Petit. W.I. Brown bands, short spines, and canal curved back. 2″ 4.50

16. *Voluta (Scaphella) junonia* Shaw. Fla. to Tex. Cream, with rows of roundish dots. Becoming scarce. To 6″. 3″ 7.00

17. *Petricola pholadiformis* Lam. Gulf of St. Law. to Gulf of Mex. and south. False Angel Wing. Elongated. Chalk white. 2″ .35

18. *Pitar dione* L. Tex. to W.I. Long spines on posterior end. Violet and purple staining. Spines seldom perfect, but often good. 1¾″—2¾″. 2″ 2.00

19. *Cymatium krebsi* Mörch. Gulf of Mex. Whitish, with light brown stains on body and last varix. Teeth on inner and outer lip. Mature specimens rare. 2¾″ 20.00

20. *Pitar lupinaria* Lesson. Baja Calif. to Peru. Fragile spines. Similar to *Pitar dione* L. (No. 18), but on West Coast. Spines seldom perfect, but often good. 2″ with spines perfect 3.50

21. *Terebellum terebellum* L. Indo-Pac. Three varying markings of this shiny fragile species. Long aperture. Scarce. 2¼″ 1.25, Scarce patterns 2.00

22. Same as No. 21.

23. Same as No. 21.

24. *Haliotis scalaris* Leach. S.W.Aust. Syn: *H. tricostalis* Lam. Back deeply sculptured. Crinkled, with pearl interior. Rare. 2¼″ 7.50

25. *Latiaxis kiranus* Kuroda. Japan White, with spiny processes. 1¼″ 7.50

26. *Volva volva* L. Japan. Shuttle Shell. Pinkish, with ends produced. 2″—3″. 2¾″ .75

27. *Ensis directus* Conrad. Labrador to

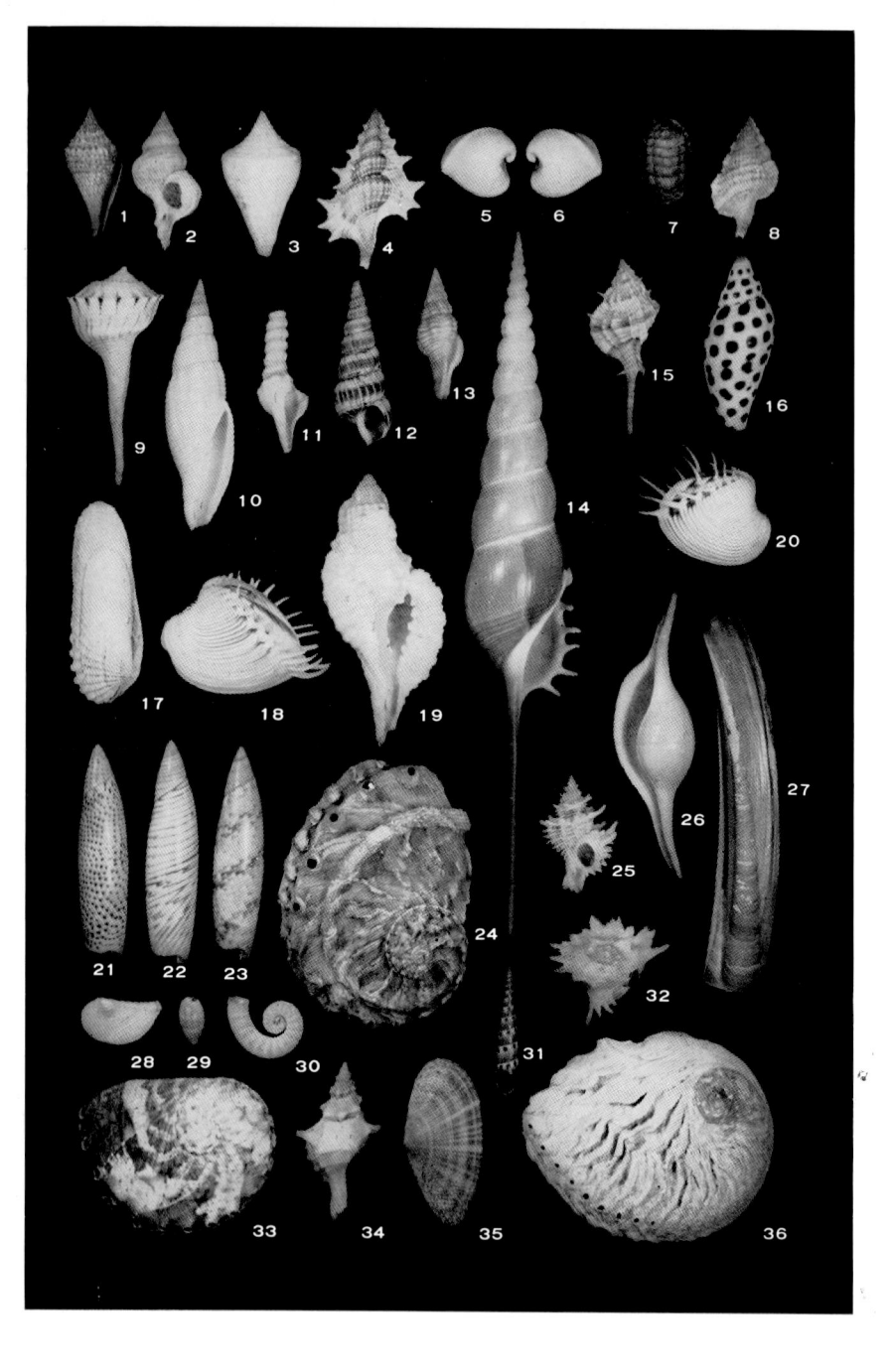

PLATE 46

Plate 46 (cont.)

S.C. Razor Clam. Long, curved, and fragile. Reaches 10″. 2″—10″. 3½″ .35

28. *Pandora gouldiana* Dall. Gulf of St. Law. to Cape May. Remarkably thin. Iridescent inside and at beaks.
1⅛″ 1.00

29. *Cypraea raysummersi* Schilder, 1960. Laminusa and Tapul Group, Sulu Archipelago. Banded cream and light brown. Purple ends. Fine teeth. Named recently after the West Coast collector, Ray Summers. ½″ 1.75

30. *Spirula spirula* L. Cape Cod to W.I. & World Seas. The cephalopod mollusk in which this interior shell is enclosed lives in deep seas and is seldom seen. The shells are cast up on beaches. 1″ .40

31. *Terebra (Hastula) diversa* Smith. Japan. Shiny grey whorls with dotted white bands.
1⅜″ .50

32. *Latiaxis pilsbryi* Hirase. Japan. White. Most spectacular of the genus. Spines at canal. Wide table-like spire with flattened spines. Rare. 1¼″ 15.00

33. *Haliotis ovina* Gmel. Polynesia. Patterned back. Inside is pearl. 2½″ .75

34. *Trophonopsis gorgon* Dall. Slim. Peach between white spined varices. 1¾″ 4.00

35. *Tellinella pulcherrima* Sow. Japan. Pink with lighter rays. Scaly at ends.
1⅝″ 1.00

36. *Haliotis midae* L. S.Afr. Odd wrinkled folds. Inside is iridescent. 4″ 2.75

Plate 47

1. *Argonauta nodosa* Sol. Aust. Paper Nautilus. One of about 20 species from warm seas. As with *Argonauta argo* L., these egg-cradles of a small octopus are scarce and fragile. The species differ chiefly in the nature of the crinkling.
2½″—8″ About 1.50 an inch

2. *Voluta (Neptuneopsis) gilchristi* Sow. S.Afr. Slim, cream to white, and always rough finish—not glossy. Rare. 6″ 18.00

3. *Xenophora pallidula* Reeve. Japan. A Carrier Shell. Dead shells are attached to the top and edge by the mollusk. Base is a pale yellow. 2″—4″ .50—2.50

4. *Tonna ringens* Swainson. Mazatlan, W. Mex. to Peru. Grinning Tun. Handsome, channeled globe. Under rock ledges at low tide. 3″—8″. 3¼″ 1.00, 6¼″ 3.50

5. *Spondylus sinensis* Schreibers. Japan. Orange-red. Odd leaflike spines.
2½″ 8.00

6. *Spondylus wrightianus ella* Ired. E.Aust. White, with four or five rows of spines, some very long. Several rows of small spines run between. 6″ across long spines 6.00

7. *Nassarius fossatus* Gould. Brit.Colum. to Calif. Light brown, with orange opening and axial ribs. Largest of genus on West Coast. 1½″ .50

8. *Cerithium nodulosum* Brug. Indo-Pac. Probably largest of the genus. Prominent nodules. Rough. 3″—5″ .50—1.25

9. *Voluta (Volutocorbis) lutosa* Koch. S. Afr. Peach color with whitish spire and circling ridges. Rough. Dredged in deep water off mouth of Orange River. Only recently described. Scarce. 2¾″ 3.00

10. *Voluta (Livonia) roadnightae* McCoy N.S.W., Aust. Cream to light pink. Fine brown lines forming lightning-like zig-zags. Baron von Mueller discovered the first known specimen, found by a Mrs. Roadnight on 90 Mile Beach, and used to prop open his window. Seldom taken alive. Good beach specimens. 5″—8″. 5½″ 18.00

11. *Fasciolaria hunteria* Perry. Fla. to W.I. Banded Tulip. Syn: *F. distans* Lam. Smooth curved whorls. Cream, with mottled grey-brown and circled by fine dark lines.
2″—4″ .50—1.00

12. *Tridacna squamosa* Lam. Pac. Furbelow Clam. White, yellow, orange, or rose, with spectacular hooded scales. Large specimens with fine frills are scarce and hard to clean of lime deposits. Can reach 10″ or more.
3″—5″ with good color and frills 1.00—5.00

13. *Tegula regina* Stearns. Calif. Tall, many-ribbed, and cone-shaped. Base is black, and opening is yellow to orange. From deep water. Scarce. Base 1½″—2″. 2″ 2.75

14. *Tridacna crocea* Lam. P.I. Close frills toward edge. Gaping side. Tinged yellow to orange-red. Porcelaneous rib-ends are peach color. Scarce. 3½″ 3.50

15. *Xenophora robusta* Verrill. W.Mex. Similar to *X. pallidula* Reeve, but carrying different shells, and it has strong orange-brown stain at aperture. Off shore in 25 fms.
2½″ 2.00

16. *Buccinum (Babylonia) japonica* Reeve. Japan. Syn: *Eburna j.* Whitish, with band of brown and curved patches, alternating with bands of brown dots. 3″ .60

17. *Turbo petholatus* L. P.I. Tapestry Shell. Graceful turban shape. Shiny, with very variable patterns and varying colors of grey, green, black, or brown. Reeve distinguished an orange variety as *T. variabilis* Reeve. Green, jewel-like operculum, or "Cat's Eye." Fine shell to set up in a color series. 1½″—3″. 1½″ .50, Bright green or orange 1.50

18. *Amphiperas ovum* L. Indo-Pac. Syn: *Ovula ovum* L. Cowry-like, egg-shaped, pure white, and porcelaneous. Reddish brown interior. Used as charms in ancient times. 1¾″—4½″. 2½″ .40, 3½″ 1.00

19. *Ficus gracilis* Sow. Pac. Pale brown. Fine spirals crossed by descending rippling lines. See also Plate 41, No. 1. 3″—6″.
5″ 2.50

20. *Perotrochus (Mikadotrochus) hirasei* Pilsbry. Japan. Emperor's Top. Syn: *Pleurotomaria hirasei* Pilsbry. Famous, much-admired slit shell. Pointed spire.

Plate 47 (cont.)

Sides sloping concavely through many whorls to a slit in the last whorl. Sweeping salmon-to-red-brown curved marks across the whorls. Pearly interior. From very deep water. Young specimens have freshest color. Rare. 2"—4". 3½" 35.00 and up

21. *Thatcheria mirabilis* Angas. Japan. The Wonder Shell. Unique cornucopia-shaped body whorl, topped by a spire ascending like a ramp to a point. Thin flaring lip. Color varies from beige to pinkish brown.

Possibly the most admired of all shells. 1½"—4" 2.00—10.00

22. *Voluta (Cymbium) olla* L. Portugal to W.Afr. Syn: *C. philipinum* Röd. Buff body. Nipple-like apex. Upper part of body whorl is rounded and deeply channeled. Flaring lip. 4" 5.00

23. *Tridacna maxima* Röd. Indo-Pac. Syns: *T. elongata* Lam., *ibid* Humphrey, and *T. noae* Röd.

PLATE 47

Plate 48

1. *Murex elenensis* Dall. W.Mex. Cream. Short spines. Lavender in aperture. 1½″—3″.   1¾″ .60

2. *Leucozonia cingulata* Lam. Baja Calif. o Peru. Syn: *Opeatostoma pseudodon* Burrow. Dark rings on white. Perhaps longest apertural tooth of any gastropod.   1¾″ 1.00

3. *Cantharus mendozana* Berry, 1959. n≥lege, W. Coast of Baja Calif. Named for collector Xavier Mendoza of Guaymas. White, with whorls ringed by pointed nodules. Scarce.   1¾″ 1.00

4. *Turris (Knefastia) tuberculifera* Brod. & Sow. ' W.Mex. Alternately banded with spiraling white nodules and dark brown bands. Rare. 1¾″—2¼″.   2″ 2.00

5. *Distorsio decussatus* Val. W.Mex. Brown staining on white. Two folds on inner lip near top end of opening.   1¾″ 1.25

6. *Conus arcuatus* Brod. & Sow. W.Mex. Brown on white. High concave spire. 1¼″—1½″.   1½″ 10.00

7. *Latirus mediamericanus* Hertlein & Strong. W.Mex. Brown axial swellings. Not common.   1½″ 1.75

8. *Phos articulatus* Hinds. W.Mex. Orange tints, with brown on axial knobs. 1¼″—1¾″.   1¼″ 3.00

9. *Turris (Knefastia) walkeri* Berry. W. Mex. Brown. The nodal ribs cross spiral cords. 1½″—1¾″.   1¾″ 1.00

10. *Fusinus ambustus* Gould. W.Mex. Brown, with darker brown on axial knobs. 1¼″—1¾″.   1¼″ .50

11. *Terebra formosa* Deshayes. W.Mex. White, with three bands of dots on body whorl. Rare. 1½″—3″.   2½″ 3.00

12. *Murex (Eupleura) muriciformis triquetra* Berry W.Mex. Greyish brown to white. Almost winged. Variable.   1½″ 1.00

13. *Murex (Eupleura) muriciformis* Brod. W.Mex.   1½″ .45

14. *Murex (Typhis) quadratus* Hinds. W. Mex. Light brown to white, with unique projecting tube on shoulder of body whorl. Rare.   ¾″ 8.50

15. *Cancellaria urceolata* Hinds. W.Mex. Brown and cancellate.   1″ 1.50

16. *Phos veraguensis* Hinds. W.Mex. Brownish and cross-ribbed.   1⅛″ 2.00

17a. *Turris (Pleuroliria) oxytropis* Sow. W. Mex. Creamy white or buff.   1″ 1.25

17b. *Turris (Pleuroliria) oxytropis albicarinata* Sow. W.Mex. Same as No. 17a, but buff with white keels.   1″ 1.25

18. *Calliostoma bonita* Strong, Hanna, & Hertlein. W.Mex. Brown. Purple channel bordering inner lip.   ¾″ 1.50

19. *Architectonica placentalis* Hinds. W. Mex. Brown and flat. Like Atlantic coast *A. peracuta* Dall. Rare.   ½″ 7.00

20. *Crucibulum serratum* Brod. W.Mex. White. Inner cup flat against shell.   ½″ 1.00

21. *Cosmioconcha palmeri* Dall. W.Mex. Shiny brown. Impressed line below suture.   ¾″ 2.00

22. *Epitonium (Eglisia) nebulosa* Dall. W. Mex. Assigned tentatively to *Eglisia*. Brownish, with fine cancellation. No varices.   ¾″ 6.00

23. *Natica broderipiana* Récluz. W.Mex. Brown, with three white bands which have brown spots. Not common.   ½″ .80

24. *Fusinus panamensis* Dall. W.Mex. White. Pointed brown-tipped knobs. Rare.   4″ 3.75

25. *Pleuroliria picta* Reeve, *ex* Beck Mss. W.Mex. White. Flecks of brown on spiral cords.   2″ 1.25

26. *Sanguinolaria tellinoides* A. Adams. Panamic Prov. Brighter red within than without.   2¼″ 1.50

27. *Mitra hindsii* Reeve. W.Mex. Beautiful and delicate. Pink, with fine brown spiral lines. Not common.   1″—1½″ 3.00

28. *Polinices helicoides* Gray, 1825. Panamic Prov. Syn: *Natica glauca* Lesson, 1830. Thin and flat. Umbilicus overhung by a tongue. Not common.   2″ 1.50

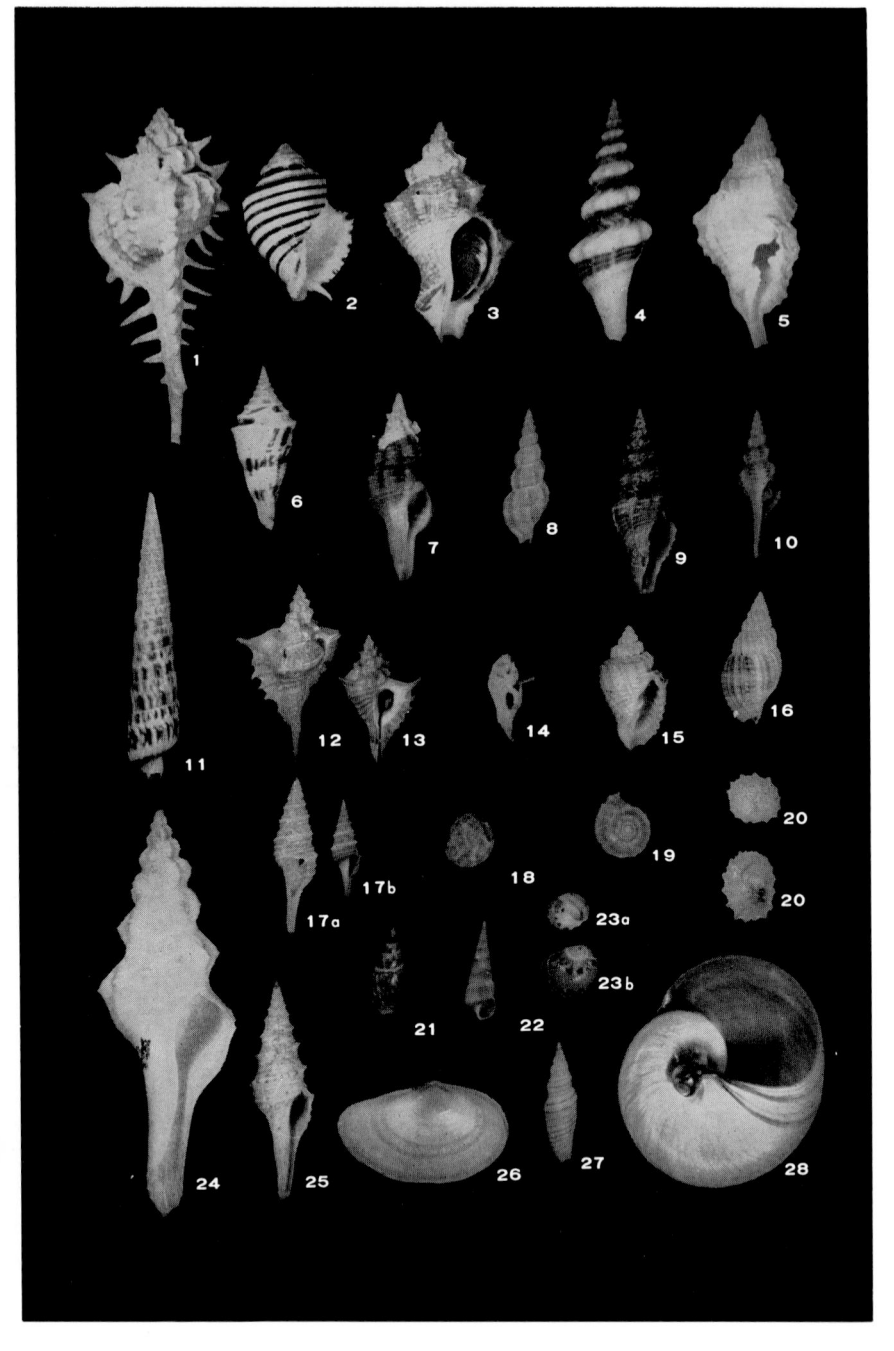

PLATE 48

Plate 49

1. *Fusinus couei* Petit. E.Mex. Graceful spindle with curved canal. White.
4″ 1.75

2. *Murex (Muricopsis) hexagonus* Lam. Fla.Keys, Cuba, & W.I. White, perhaps with tints of orange-brown. Ribs are spinose. 1″—1½″. 1¼″ 2.00

3. *Cypraea cinerea* Gmel. Cuba & W.I. Brownish, perhaps with black-brown specks. Base is cream, perhaps with brown between teeth. ¾″—1½″. 1″ 1.00

4. *Epitonium scalare* L. E.Aust. & Pac. Syn: *E. pretiosa* Lam. Precious Wentletrap (Spiral Staircase). A favorite for centuries. The globelike whorls hardly touch one another. Thin bladelike ribs. Once counterfeited by Chinese artisans in rice flour.
1½″ 3.50, 2″ 6.00 and up

5. *Conus austini* Rehder & Abbott. Fla. to Yucatan. Usually white. The odd-sized spiral thread on the sides is a characteristic. Shoulder is sharp or rounded. 1¼″ 2.00

6. *Turris (Polystira) albida* Perry. Campeche, E.Mex. White and corded. 2¾″—4″.
2¾″ 1.25

7. *Conus praecellens* A. Adams. Japan. White, with brown markings. Sloping spire. See also Plate 43, No. 31.
1¼″ 2.00

8. *Turris filograna* Odhner. Senegal, W. Afr. Dredged. Spiny at shoulders of spire. Rare. 1″ 3.50

9. *Aporrhais senegalensis* Gray. Senegal, W. Afr. Typical flaring spines of this genus, but much smaller than *A. pes-pelicani* L.
⅝″ 2.50

10. *Murex cailleti kugleri* Clench & Farfante. B.W.I. Small stocky shell with short spines. 1½″ 3.50

11. *Turris (Clavatula) sacerdos* Reeve. Senegal, W.Afr. Short canal. Uncommon.
1″ 1.25

12. *Cassis (Sconsia) striata* Lam. Campeche, E.Mex. Rows of brown sickles or half-moons. Usually has fine incised lines. From deep water. Rare. 1½″—2¾″.
1⅞″ 2.50

13. *Turris undatiruga* Bivona. Med.Sea to Senegal, W.Afr. Dredged. Beige swirling varices which are raised at shoulders.
1⅜″ 1.50

14. *Conus mitratus* Hwass. P.I. Syn: *C. mitraeformis* Sow. Resembles a mitre. Lip curved. Brown stripes. 1″ 4.50

15. *Terebra senegalensis* Lam. Senegal, W. Afr. Circles of irregular patching.
3¼″ 2.50

16. *Murex pinnatus* Swain. China Coast. Distinctive. Dainty triangular white species.
2½″ 12.00

17. *Cypraea spurca acicularis* Gmel. W. I. Fulvous to orange dorsum with pale lateral spots. Fulvous ¾″ .75, orange ¾″ 1.50

18a and 18b. *Murex decussatus* Gmel. Senegal, W.Afr. & Brazil. Unusual form with dark marking. Some believe its occurrence on both sides of the Atlantic is due to currents. 1¼″ 3.50

19. *Turritella (Mesalia) brevialis* Lam. Senegal, W.Afr. Ash color. 2″ 2.00

20. *Murex (Tritonalia) fasciatus* Sow. Senegal, W.Afr. Dredged. 1¼″ 2.50

21. *Conus genuanus* Hwass. Senegal, W. Afr. Distinctive circling of brown dots and hyphens. Rare. 2″ Fine, live-caught 20.00

22. *Eucrassatella speciosa* A. Adams, 1853. Gulf of Mex. Gibb's Clam. Syn: *Crassatella gibbsii* Tuomey & Holmes, 1856. Dredged in 100 fms. Orange and brownish rays on white concentric ridges. 1⅜″ 1.50

23a and 23b. *Pecten benedicti* Verrill & Bush. S.Fla. & Gulf of Mex. Bright shades of brown to orange, and occasionally lemon. ⅝″ 2.00 and up

24. *Conus rainesae* McGinty. Tampa Bay. Dredged in 65 fms. Cream, with high pointed spire. Rare. About ¾″ 50.00

25. *Conus villepinii fosteri* Clench and Aguayo. Tampa Bay. Dredged in 9 fms. White, high pointed, scaliform spire. Bands of brown splotches or patches. Rare.
15/16″ 15.00 and up

PLATE 49

Plate 49 (cont.)

26. *Chione latilirata* Conrad. Tampa Bay. Imperial Venus. Dredged in 15 fms. Deep cutting causing five or six shelved or swollen ridges. Cream, rayed and mottled with brown. Uncommon. 1″ 3.00

27. *Murex cabriti* Bernardi. Tampa Bay. Dredged in moderately deep water. Drab white, but fresh specimens may be pink. "A collector's item." 2⅝″ 8.00 and up

28. *Fusinus eucosmius* Dall. Tampa Bay. Dredged in 58 fms. Swollen white axial varices. Deep water specimens have orange between ribs. Spire is bent. "A collector's item." 2¼″ 9.00 and up

29. *Voluta (Volutocorbis) abyssicola* Adams & Reeve. S.Afr. Deep cream to orange-brown. Whorls of swelling curves cross-netted with ridges. 2¾″ 30.00

30. *Epitonium (Claviscala) kuroharai* Kuroda. Japan. Long and terebra-like. Curved swollen varices or ribs. 2¾″ 7.00

31. *Murex beaui* Fisher & Bernardi. Tampa Bay. Dredged in 80 fms. White and pellucid. In the rare deep water specimens, webbed edges of aperture look like semi-transparent fins. Varices are similarly webbed, but seldom remain beyond the body whorl. High spire and deep sutures. Webbed aperture. 3″ 15.00 and up, With webbed varices also—40.00 and up

Plate 50

1. *Haliotis fulgens* Philippi. S.Calif. to N. Mex. Blue-green Abalone. A favorite because of its size, to 8″, and because of its iridescent interior. There are many attractive Ear Shells widely scattered in world seas. *Haliotis rufescens* Swain (Red Abalone) to 12″, dull brick red outside, somewhat like *H. fulgens* inside. Both have rough, perhaps wormy back except in selected specimens. 6″—8″ 1.00—1.50, With backs polished to fine color 5.00 and up.

2. *Cardium costatum* L. W.Afr. Ribbed Cockle. Ivory, with dark brown between largest of the strongly keeled ribs. Valves gape on heart-shaped side. 3½″ 3.50

3. *Lambis chiragra* L. E.Ind. to Polynesia. Beautiful mottled brown on cream. Aperture flushed with orange-brown. Smooth lower columella. Six large hooked canals. This large form is a female. Male forms are similar, but smaller, and may resemble *Lambis arthritica* Röd. *L. rugosa* Sow. with a reddish aperture, is said to be an uncommon form of the male of *L. Chiragra*. 8½″ 2.50

4. *Voluta (Melo) amphora* Sol. N.E. Aust. Baler or Melon Shell. Syns: *V. (Melo) diadema* Lam. and *V. (Melo) flammea* Röd. Cream to pink, with some tenting and banding. Swollen aperture extended above spire. To 18″. 5″ 1.50, 8″ 4.50

5. *Malleus albus* Lam. P.I. Similar to M. *anatina* Lam., but hammer-shaped. Fragile crinkled bivalve. 4″—7″ 1.25—2.50

6. *Nautilus pompilius* L. Sulu Sea, P.I. Chambered Nautilus. One of the most famous and curious of shells. Written about extensively in articles and books. Found in most collections. 6″ 2.50, Pearled 5.00, Split halves 5½″ 1.25—2.25

7. *Voluta (Melo) aethiopica* L. N.E.Aust. & P.I. Syn: *Melo broderipi* Grey. Wide aperture. Scalelike spines circle the spire. Yellow-brown, with some banding. May reach 12″. 7½″ 4.50

8. *Fusus dupetitthouarsi* Kiener. W.Mex. to Ecuador. Found in mud flats at low tide. White. One of the largest of the genus and may reach 10″. 4½″—9″ 1.00—3.00

9. *Strombus galeatus* Swain Mex. to Ecuador. One of heaviest West American gastropods. Young shells are conical. Mature ones with thick flaring lip. Light brown, with ivory interior. Spire often corroded. 7½″ Young 1.00, Mature 3.00

PLATE 50

Plate 51

1. *Codakia orbicularis* L. Fla. to E.Mex. Crossing radial and concentric threads give a beaded effect. Inside is white to pale yellow. Edge by hinge is sometimes rose. Used for food. 2½" .30

2. *Dosinia discus* Reeve. Va. to W.I. White and disk-shaped. Like *D. elegans*, but less circular, more, and finer ridges, 50 per inch in adults. 2"—3". 2½" .50

3. *Venus mercenaria* L. Gulf of St.Law. to Gulf of Mex. Dull white, with purple staining inside. Triangular-ovate. Swollen. Eaten as "Quahog," "Cherrystone Clam," and "Little Neck Clam." 3"—5" .50—1.00

4. *Rangia cuneata* Gray. Fla. to E.Mex. Edible mollusk. Thick and wedge-shaped. From banks by brackish streams. Olive periostracum. Eroded at umbones. 1¾" .50

5. *Megapitaria aurantiaca* Sow. W.Mex. to Ecuador. Among largest of *Veneridae*. Shiny red-brown periostracum on thick pinkish shell. Inside, white hinge-plate has a purple tint. Not common. To over 4". 2¾" 1.25, 3¾" 2.00

6. *Anomia simplex* Orb. Cape Cod to W.I. Translucent yellow to orange. Upper valve is concave, and lower is convex with hole. 1½" .25

7. *Dosinia dunkeri* Philippi. W.Mex. to Peru. Cream. Circular, with fine concentric ribs. 2½" .75

8. *Dosinia bilunulata* Gray. Japan. Disc-like and shiny. Fine concentric lines crossed by brownish rays. Sharp serrations on both anterior edges. 3" .75

9. *Modiolus demissus* Dillwyn. Gulf of St. Law. to N.C. & introduced into Calif. Syns: *Volsella plicatulatus* Lam. and *Mytilis plicatulus* Lam. Brown to black, with pearly, bluish white inside and brownish stains. Many bifurcating ribs. Not usually regarded as edible since it grows best in polluted waters. 2"—4". 2½" .25

10. *Malleus anatinus* Lam. P.I. Fragile, translucent, crinkled "Beak" and black inner patch showing through like an "eye" give this the name Duck Hammer. Usually encrusted. 3¾" 2.00

11. *Venus (Paphia) euglypta* Phil. Japan. Shiny pink-brown, with rays of brown patches. Neat concentric cords. 3" .65

12. *Cardita affinis* Sow. W.Mex. Elongated, with heavy ribs and dark patches on one half of valve, smoothing to yellowish on other half. 2½" .50

13. *Venus (Macrocallista) maculata* L. N.C. to Brazil. Calico Shell or Checkerboard. Subovate and shiny. Regular roughly-squarish patches of red-brown on cream or pink. 2½" .75

14. *Placunanomia cumingii* Brod. W.Mex. to Ecuador. Pink to white. Radially crinkled forming zig-zag edges. Showy, but not common in collections. Largest of the Jingle Shells. 3" 2.50

15. *Venus (Megapitaria) squalida* Sow. W. Mex. to Peru. Shiny, with grey-brown periostracum. Shell is grey-brown, and white inside. To 5". 2½" .75

16. *Lima lima* L. Pac. Pure white, with sharp scales on radiating ribs. 2½" .75

17. *Dosinia elegans* Conrad. N.C. to Yucatan. Sub-circular white, fine, concentric rings, about 20-25 per inch in adults. Beaks are high and pointing forward. To 2¾". 2" .50

18. *Venus (Macrocallista) bardwelli* Clench & McClean. E.Afr. Flesh color. Shiny brown rays curve across flattened cords. 3" 1.00

19. *Venus (Callista) chinensis* Holten. Japan. Shiny, with buff-brown raised cords at edge widening to apex. Channeled. Rays sometimes purpled. 2½"—3". 2½" .50

20. *Venus (Periglypta) multicostata* Sow. Mex. to Peru. Heavy, white, and squarish with corners rounded. Ribs crossing high concentric ridges produce a textile-like effect. Violet under hinge. To 4¼". 3" 1.00

PLATE 51

Plate 52

1. *Cardium (Clinocardium) nuttallii* Conrad. Calif. to Bering Sea & Japan. White. Heavy ribs. Common edible Basket Cockle. 2″—6″.   2½″ .50

2. *Venus (Ventricolaria) isocardia* Verrill. W.Mex. to Colombia. Grey-brown, with dark blotches. Heavy, ridged, concentric ribs. A "dent" in one side.   3″ 2.50

3. *Cardium (Trachycardium) consors* Sow. W.Mex. to Ecuador. Handsome in form and color. Buffs, pinks, and browns. Heavy ribs which, on the "heart" side, have scales that look like overlapping rings.
2″ 1.25

4. *Hippopus maculatus* Lam. Pac. Syn: *H. hippopus* L. Young shells are cream to yellow, with red-brown spots. Larger shells pale out. Unique shape. A thick shell with heavy ribs and a flattened side, making its form merit the common name of Bear's Paw. 2″—9″.   3″ .40, 6½″ 2.50

5. *Cyrtopleura costata* L. Mass. to W.I. Angel Wing. White. Each valve is somewhat triangular, with complicated diverging ribs. When alive the valves are held together by a hinge covered with an extra part, a shelly accessory plate or "bridge." Complete specimens with all the parts are relatively scarce. The whole shell is fragile. 6¼″ Matched, unattached pairs with bridge 2.25

6. *Ostrea crista-galli* Linné. Pac. Cock's Comb. Brown. Extraordinary form, which photographs poorly. Reeve wrote of it: "Folds angular and deep." Not common.
2¾″ 2.00

7. *Arca (Anadara) lienosa floridana* Conrad. N.C. to Fla. Cut-Ribbed Ark. White. Dark periostracum. Has 30-38 ribs, each divided by a fine line. Incorrectly called *Arca secticostata* Reeve. Not very common. 2½″—5″.   2¾″ 1.00

8. *Glycymeris gigantea* Reeve. Gulf of Calif. to Acapulco. White, patched with brown and streaked with radial striae. About 30 hinge teeth. Especially attractive if polished.   Natural 3″ 1.75
Polished 2½″ 2.75

9. *Arca (Anadara) ovalis* Brug. Cape Cod to W.I. Blood Ark. In some books, identified as *Arca pexata* Say. White, with dark periostracum. About 26-35 ribs which are broader than interlines. One of the few mollusks with red blood.   1¼″ .40

10. *Arca (Anadara) multicostata* Sow. Calif. to Panama. Many-Ribbed Ark. A striking stocky shell with a dark periostracum. Thick and squarish, with 26-31 ribs. 3″—4″.   3¾″ 1.00

11. *Cardium (Dinocardium) robustum* Sol. Va. to E.Mex. Great Heart Cockle. Straw-colored, with posterior slope mahogany-red shading to purple near the edge. 32-36 ribs. 3″—4″. A variety of this, *Dinocardium robustum vanhyningi* Clench & L. C. Smith is found where this one is not, in S.W. Fla. from Tampa Bay to Cape Sable. The variety is more elongated, glossier, and more colorful. To 5″. Higher than it is long.
Both types 3½″ .50

12. *Venus (Meretrix) meretrix lusoria* Röd. Japan. Shiny, with fascinating differences in markings and in colors which vary from brown through cream, white, yellow, and bluish to grey.   2″ .50

13. *Chama lazarus* L. Indo-Pac. Whitish, with some color staining. Many flat fronds. Found on coral reefs, one valve solidly attached to reef and so not easily removable.
3½″ 3.00

Plate 52

Plate 53

1. *Epitonium (Amaea) magnifica* Sow. Japan. Huge for an *Epitonium*. White and graceful. Rare. ³⁄₄″ 9.00, 4¹⁄₄″ 12.00

2. *Fusinus irregularis* Grabau. Outer coast of Baja Calif. Narrow, long, curved canal. Rare. 5³⁄₄″ 2.50

3. *Fusinus turriculus* Kiener. Hong Kong. Swollen varices. 3¹⁄₂″ 3.50

4. *Fusinus longicaudus* Bory. E.Afr. Raised lines at periphery of early whorls. Long canal. Brown. 4³⁄₄″ 1.25

5. *Fusinus nicobaricus* Lam. Pac. Patching of brown. 3¹⁄₂″ 1.25

6. *Fusinus tuberculatus* Lam. E.Afr. Nodulation on shoulders. Brownish canal. 3¹⁄₂″ 1.75

7. *Cassis (Morum) grande* A. Adams. Japan. Wide lip and flaring columella. Much prized. Rare. 2¹⁄₂″ 12.00

8. *Vasum tubiferum* Anton. P.I. Syn: *V. imperialis* Reeve. Imperial Vase. Strong spines. Deep, funnel-like umbilicus. Purplish spots on parietal wall.
2¹⁄₂″—4¹⁄₂″ 4.00—8.00

9. *Cardita inguinata* Nickles. Senegal. W. Afr. Layered ridges. 1¹⁄₄″ 3.25

10. *Venus chevreuxi* Dante. Senegal, W. Afr. Dredged. Rare. 1¹⁄₂″ 4.00

11. *Syrinx aruanus* L. N.Aust. Syn: *Megalatractus proboscidifera* Lam. Yellowish. Thin for its size. Larger specimens lose the unusual nucleus. Vies with *Fasciolaria gigantea* Kiener of West Indies for reputation as largest gastropod. May reach 24″ so becoming very heavy, but best ones are 15″—16″. Larger ones lose the usual nucleus. See Plate 46, No. 11.
4¹⁄₂″ 3.00, 10″ 7.00

12. *Conus ichinoseana* Kuroda Japan. Patterned with brown dots and flecks on white.
2¹⁄₄″ 8.50

13. *Macron aethiops* Reeve. W.Mex. White, with dark green periostracum.
2³⁄₄″ 2.50

14. *Rapa rapa* L. Sulu Sea, P.I. Unusual bulbous form. Fragile. 2″ 1.75

15. *Murex stainforthi* Reeve. N.W.Aust. Stocky. Ribs are bright tan, and aperture is orange-pink. 2″ 1.75

16. *Murex brevifrons* Lam. Cuba & B.W.I. Resembles *M. ramosus* Lam., but smaller and more delicate. Cream to dark brown.
3″ 2.50

17. *Fusinus panamensis* Dall. W.Mex. to Ecuador. White, with 8 whorls and 9-10 axial ribs. Rare. 3″ 3.50

18. *Conus dalli* Stearns. W.Panama. Tented or waved pattern. Browns, yellows, and darker bands. Aperture is peach. Belongs to the group of Textile Cones. Scarce. 2″ 3.50

19. *Conus zonatus* Hwass. Andaman & Maldive Islands. Brilliant pattern of dark banding and marking on white. See Plate 21, No. 8. 2″ 26.00

20. *Cymatium poulsenii* Mörch. Campeche & W.I. Syn: *C. cingulatum peninsulum* Maxwell Smith. Stocky, broad, plump varices. Very rare. 2³⁄₄″ 20.00 and up

21. *Cassis sophia* Brazier. N.S.W., Aust. Round and swollen. White, with rows of chestnut blotches. Rare. 2³⁄₄″ 6.00

22. *Xenophora digitata* Mart. Senegal, W. Afr. Scarce. Dredged in deep water. Rare.
2¹⁄₂″ 15.00

23. *Strombus taurus* Reeve. Marshall Is. Characteristic spurs extending above aperture. Found in pairs on Rongelap and Eniwetok Islands. Rare. 3¹⁄₂″ 35.00

PLATE 53

Plate 54

1. *Conus tulipa* L. Indo-Pac. A poisonous cone. Background is bluish white, with longitudinal red-purple waving and fine encircling lines of white dotted with brown. Aperture is purplish. The shell is thin and light, with a low spire, slightly coronated. 2½″   2.75

2. *Conus tigrinus* Sow. Indo-Pac. Possible Syn: *C. textile* L. Reddish brown, with tentlike markings, some of which are very tiny, others up to ¼″. Inside is pink. 2⅛″   3.00

3. *Conus trigonus* Reeve. N.W.Aust. Light and dark yellow bands, with white band at middle and tip. 2″   4.00

4. *Fusinus timessus* Dall. Gulf of Mex. White, with spiral cording. Roundish aperture and flaring parietal wall. 4½″   14.00

5. *Cypraea coxeni hesperina* Schilder & Summers. New Brit. Smaller than *C. coxeni* Cox, and spots on dorsum are darker and tend to blend into blotches rather than appear as freckles. ¾″   5.00

6. *Fusinus perplexus* A. Adams. Japan. White, with well separated spiral cords. Tip and waved canal are beige. 4½″   1.00

7. *Conus flavidus* Lam. Pac. Syn: *C. neglectus* Pease. Yellow-brown, with narrow white banding near middle. Aperture is deep purple. Rounded shoulder and flat top. Uncoronated spire distinguishes this from *Conus lividus* Hwass. A color difference may also be observed, tending to yellow in *C. flavidus* and to olive-green in *C. lividus*. 2″   1.00

8. *Conus stercusmuscarum* L. Indo-Pac. Syn: *C. arenatus* Röd. Fly-Spotted Cone. White, encircled with black dots which sometimes are close together, forming patches. Deep pink in aperture. Smooth rounded form. Spire felt with finger has no small nodules like *C. arenatus* Hwass which is also stockier and has smaller dots. 2″   1.25

9. *Conus caracteristicus* G. Fisher. Pac. Syn: *C. characteristicus* Dillwyn. White,

with three bands of wavy brown lines. Small, triangular, brown spotting. Spire is flat, and apex is elevated. Heavy. 1¾″   2.25

10. *Cypraea caput-draconis* Melvill. Easter Island. Dark, with humped dorsum and uniformly small specks. Bluish-grey terminal blotches. Depressed margins. Scarce. 1⅛″   5.00

11. *Mitra vulpecula* Lam. Indo-Pac. Very variable, but often orange-brown with dark brown banding. High spire, with raised ribbing. Almost always with black patch where parietal wall meets top of lip. 1¾″   .75

12. *Mitra granosa* Chem. Pac. Syns: *M. sanguisuga* Lam. and *M. stigmataria* Lam. Greyish, sometimes with a few of the beads red. Beads formed by crossing of spiral lines and rounded axial ribs. Dark aperture. 1½″   1.00

13. *Mitra regina filiareginae* J. Cate. Samar, 1961. P.I. Lacks the bright color variation of *M. regina* Sow. Mostly whitish, with black bands, but usually a peach tint near shoulder of body whorl and about aperture. 2¼″   4.00

14. *Conus princeps* L. Gulf of Calif. to Ecuador. Orange-pink, with dark brown wavy axial stripes. In the variety *C. p. lineolatus* Val., the stripes are merely fine lines. To about 2″. 1½″   2.50

15. *Cymatium femorale* L. S.E.Fla. to W.I. Light brown to reddish orange. Larger spiral cords end in nodules on flaring lip. Sharply angular at top. 3″—7″. 3¾″   3.50

16. *Voluta (Cymbiolacca) complexa* Ired. Queensland, Aust. Syn: *V. punctata* Swain. Pinkish tan. Smooth and shiny. Almost oval. Slightly darker, large, squarish patches tending to bands. Whole shell sprinkled over with small dark brown dots. Shoulders of whorls with pointed nodules. Columella has four plaits. 2¼″   12.00

17. *Voluta (Volutoconus) bednalli* Brazier. Torres Straits, Aust. Unique in form and marking. Usually found only in important

PLATE 54

Plate 54 (cont.)

collections. Cream color and faintly yellowed. A beautiful over-all network of dark lines and irregular creamy patches is formed by narrow black bands connected by descendingly waved or S-shaped lines. To 6". Very rare. 3½" 100.00

18. *Voluta (Harpulina) lapponica* L. Ind. Oc. Syn: *V. loroisi* Val. Ivory, overlaid with spiral, chestnut-colored, linear hyphens. Bands of larger waved blotches, Seven plaits on columella. 2½" 8.50

19. *Clavagella ramosa* Dunker. Japan. One of the Watering Pots. An odd bivalve of which one or both of its tiny valves becomes cemented to a shelly tube which is often encrusted with sand and debris. The tube usually has a perforated disk anteriorly attached and surrounded by a fringe of calcareous tubercles. 2½" 5.00

20. *Conus patricius* Hinds, 1843. W. Nicaragua to Ecuador. Syn: *C. pyriformis* Reeve, 1843, but published by Reeve a month later than Hinds. Often a yellowed pink. Graceful pear-shaped. To 5". 3" 2.00

21. *Conus sugimotonis* Kuroda. Japan. All white, but light tan periostracum. Low spire sloping to square shoulder. Body whorl sloping down to tip almost straight, but medially slightly concave. 3½" 18.00

22. *Conus tendineus* Hwass. E.Afr. Dark brown, banded with squarish white patches. Slender, elongated, and circled by fine ridges. 2¾" 10.00

23. *Conus scalaris* Val. W.Mex. South to Acapulco. Staircase Cone. Unusually graceful because of the high, concavely sloping, stepped spire and the elongated, slightly concave body. White, banded with tan flammules. Keen says this intergrades with *C. gradatus* Wood. 1⅝" 5.00, 2½" 10.00

24. *Conus imperialis viridulus* Lam. E.Afr. Variety with little banding, but rather wide, waved, descending brown stripes against greyish white. 2½" 2.00

25. *Conus sieboldi* Reeve. Japan. White with pale-brown flammules. See Plate 45 Nos. 1 and 5. 2¼"—3½". 2¾" 1.00

GLOSSARY

TERMS

Anterior end: In a bivalve, the end opposite to that at which the ligament is attached. The front end when the mollusk moves about during life.

Aperture: Opening to the interior of a shell.

Attenuated: Drawn out or slender.

Axis: Imaginary line around which a shell coils and grows.

Base: Flat side with aperture of a Cowry.

Beach: Shell not caught alive but found on the beach.

Bivalve: Mollusk with two parts to its shell, like a clam.

Callus: Enamel-like deposit.

Chevron: Mark shaped like a "V."

Columella: Column formed at the interior axis of a univalve.

Cord: Raised spiral process of a shell, resembling a cord.

Crenulation: Regularly-notched edging.

Crown: Crownlike spiral ring on the spire.

Cuticle: Skin, membrane, or integument.

Denticle: Small, tooth-like process.

Dorsum: Back of a univalve shell on the side opposite to the aperture.

Flammule: Flame-like marking.

Frond: Leaf-like or fern-like process.

Fusiform: Spindle-shaped.

Gastropod: One of the large class of univalves called *Gastropoda*, loosely called snails.

Granule: Grain-like elevations on a shell.

Indo-Pacific: Location of shells which are widely dispersed in parts of both the Indian and Pacific Oceans.

Lip: Edge of the aperture in a univalve shell.

Lirae: Lines of a thread-like sculpture.

Nacre: Shelly matter of mother-of-pearl appearance.

Nodule: Knob-like projection.

Nucleus: First formed portion of a shell to emerge from the egg.

Operculum: Shelly or horny door of a univalve shell.

Ovate: Oval in shape.

Papule: Pimple-like process.

Parietal shield: Shield-shaped inside wall of the aperture in some shells.

Parietal wall: Inside wall of a shell, opposite the aperture.

Penultimate: Previous to the last whorl.

Periostracum: Outermost layer of a shell, usually a skin of tough material. Regarded as a more accurate term than "epidermis."

Periphery: The keel or outer portion of a shell at its greatest circumference.

Plait: Sculpturing of a shell which appears like a fold.

Pyriform: Pear-shaped.

Race: Loosely applied to a group of shells that have developed in some specific locality or under a single set of conditions.

Reticulate: Resembling a network.

Rib: Rib-shaped process.

Scalariform: Having a separation of the whorls of the shell and looking like a ladder mounting up around the shell.

Serration: Formation resembling the teeth of a saw.

Shoulder: Portion of a shell where the body whorl meets the spire.

Sinus: Spot which appears scooped out, as a growth line, or a spot on a shell where the flesh of the animal was attached.

Spire: Entire univalve shell except for the body whorl.

Striae: Sculpturing that appears like fine lines or grooves.

Subovate: Somewhat egg-shaped.

Suture: Spiral line at the junction of whorls.

Tent: Tent-shaped marking.

Tessellated: Checkered.

Truncated: Sharply or squarely cut off.

Tubercle: Small knob-like protuberance.

Type Species: Species selected, theoretically, because it has the general characteristics of the mollusks of its genus.

Umbilicus: Depression or opening in the curling interior axis of a shell, sometimes vestigial and sometimes wide.

Umbo: Upper or earliest part of a bivalve shell as seen from the outside.

Univalve: Mollusk with a shell in one part, like a snail.

Varix: Raised rib on a univalve shell corresponding to the rest period in which the animal and shell stop growing.

Whorl: One complete revolution of a spiral shell.

Wing: Part of a shell shaped like a wing. Usually seen on either side of the hinge on Pectinidae or at the outer lip of some univalves.

AUTHORS

Ad. & Rev.: Adams and Reeve

Auch.: Auchincloss

Bart. Bartsch

Brod.: Broderip

Brod & Sow: Broderip and Sowerby

Brug.: Bruguière

Carp.: Carpenter

Chem.: Chemnitz

Dautz.: Dautzenberg

Dill.: Dillwyn

d'Orb.: d'Orbigny

Ducl.: Duclos

Esch.: Eschscholtz

Gmel.: Gmelin

Ired.: Iredale

Kien.: Kiener

L.: Linné

Lam.: Lamarck

Less.: Lessing

Mart.: Martyn

Meusch.: Meuschen

Orb.: d'Orbigny

Phil.: Philippi

R. & A.: Rehder and Abbott

Rod.: Röding

Rve.: Reeve

Q. & G.: Quoy and Gaimard

Sow.: Sowerby

Swain.: Swainson

BOOK LIST

The books in this list have been selected from many because they are of use to collectors according to their interests and, in addition, are currently in print.

Abbott, R. T.: *American Sea Shells*, D. Van Nostrand Co., Inc., Princeton, N.J. 541 pp. 40 plates, 24 in color, numerous text figures. Large, fine book for serious students.

Abbott, R. T. & Warmke, G.: *Carribean Sea Shells*, Livingston Publishing Co., Narbeth, Pa. 345 pp. 44 plates, 4 in color, 34 text figures. A fine work.

Abbott, R. T.: *How to Know American Marine Shells*, Signet Key Book Co., New York, N.Y. 222 pp. 12 plates in color, 402 figures. Paperback.

Abbott, R. T. (ed.).: *Indo-Pacific Mollusca.* Available by subscription from Department of Mollusca, Academy of Sciences of Philadelphia, Philadelphia, Pa. Published continuously. Vol. I, Nos. 1–5 published to date. Monographs of marine mollusca of the Indo-Pacific (East Africa to Polynesia). Scientific series for serious students.

Abbott, R. T.: *Introducing Sea Shells*, D. Van Nostrand Co., Inc., Princeton, N.J. 64 pp. 10 plates, some in color. For beginners.

Abbott, R. T.: *Sea Shells of the World*, Golden Press, New York, N.Y. 160 pp. 500 shells in color. Useful paperback.

Allen, Joyce.: *Australian Shells*, Charles T. Branford Co., Boston, Mass. 470 pp. 12 plates in color, 28 plates in black-and-white, 110 text figures. Superb on Australian shells.

Allen, Joyce.: *Cowry Shells of World Seas*, Charles T. Branford Co., Boston, Mass. 170 pp. Many plates, some in color. Only available book on Cowries.

Bousfield, E. L.: *Canadian Atlantic Sea Shells*, National Museum of Canada, Ottawa, Canada. 72 pp. 133 figures. Common, intertidal species.

Cameron, Roderick.: *Shells*. G. P. Putnam's Sons, New York, N.Y. 128 pp. Hundreds of photos, some in color.

Clench, William (ed.).: *Johnsonia—Monographs of the Marine Shells of the Western Atlantic.* Available by subscription from Department of Mollusca, Museum of Comparative Zoology, Harvard University, Cambridge, Mass. Published continuously. Vol. I–IV published to date.

Grau, G.: *Pectinidae of the Eastern Pacific,* University of Southern California Press, Los Angeles, Calif. 308 pp. 57 plates.

Habe, T.: *The Shells of Japan in Color,* Hoikusha Publishing Co., Osaka, Japan. No. 2 in series. 103 pp. Many plates in color. Scientific names in Latin, text in Japanese.

Hirase, S. & Taki, I.: *An Illustrated Handbook of Shells from Japanese Islands and their Adjacent Territory.* Maruzen Co., Ltd., Tokyo, Japan. 134 plates, 130 in color. Scientific names in Latin, text in Japanese.

Johnstone, Y.: *Sea Treasure,* Houghton Mifflin Co., Boston, Mass. 242 pp. 8 plates in color. Enjoyable reading about shells.

Keen, Myra.: *Sea Shells of Tropical West America,* Stanford University Press, Stanford, Calif. 619 pp. 10 plates in color, 1037 figures. Definitive. A superb scientific book arranged well for collectors.

Kennelly, D. H.: *Marine Shells of Southern Africa,* Thomas Nelson & Sons, London.

Kira, T.: *Japanese Shells in Color,* Hoikusha Publishing Co., Osaka, Japan. No. 1 in series (see Habe above). 172 pp. 67 plates in color. Scientific names in Latin, text in Japanese.

Kira, T.: *Shells of the Western Pacific,* Hoikusha Publishing Co., Osaka, Japan. A larger edition, with some revisions, of Kira's *Japanese Shells in Color,* with the text in English. A handsome book but very expensive.

Marsh, J. A. & Rippingale, O. H.: *Cone Shells of the World,* Jacaranda Press, Brisbane, Australia.

McMichael, D. F.: *Some Common Shells of the Australian Sea Shore,* Jacaranda Press, Brisbane, Australia. 127 pp. 287 figures.

Melvin, A. Gordon.: *Gem Shells of World Oceans,* Naturegraph Publishing Co., Healdsburg, Calif. 96 pp. 14 plates in color. The text comments on each shell and provides the basic information needed by a collector.

Melvin, A. Gordon.: *Nautilus,* Naturegraph Publishing Co., Healdsburg, Calif. A sea-shell card game played with color cards showing the same shells shown in *Gem Shells of World Oceans.*

Morris, Percy A.: *A Field Guide to the Shells of Our Atlantic and Gulf Coasts,*

Houghton Mifflin Co., Boston, Mass. 236 pp. 45 fine plates, 8 in color. Useful.

Morris, Percy A.: *A Field Guide to the Shells of the Pacific Coast and Hawaii*, Houghton Mifflin Co., Boston, Mass. 220 pp. 40 plates, some in color. Clear photos and helpful comment.

Powell, A. W. B.: *Shells of New Zealand*, Whitcombe and Tombs, Christchurch, New Zealand. 202 pp. 36 plates, 2 in color, check list. Useful paperback.

Rogers, J. E.: *The Shell Book*, Charles T. Branford Co., Boston, Mass. 485 pp. 87 plates, 8 in color. A 1951 reprint of a 1908 edition of a popular book on shells.

Wagner, J. L. & Abbott, R. T.: *Standard Catalog of Shells*, D. Van Nostrand Co., Princeton, N.J.

Webb, Walter F.: *Foreign Land Shells*, Lee Publications, Wellesley Hills, Mass. 1,400 species in black-and-white. Only available book on land shells.

Webb, Walter F.: *Handbook for Shell Collectors*, Lee Publications, Wellesley Hills, Mass. 264 pp. Over 2,000 marine species in black-and-white. A compendium of foreign shells. Still in print many years after original publication. This book shows more photographs of *Conidae* than any other available book.

Webb, Walter F.: *Recent Mollusca*, Lee Publications, Wellesley Hills, Mass. 1,225 illustrations in black-and-white. Used for over a decade, it is still helpful. It shows shell prices as they were a long time ago. Paperback.

Wilber, K. M. & Yonge, C. M.: *Physiology of Mollusca*, Academic Press, New York, N.Y. Technical study for those who develop an interest in scientific malacology.

INDEX

The first number gives the page; the second in italic type the caption number

annettae, Cardium   100 : *4*
  ,,   , Cypraea   28 : *28*
annulata, Oliva   40 : *16* & 42 : *36*
annulus, Cypraea   26 : *8*
Anomia simplex   124 : *6*
antiguus, Magilus   84 : *26*
antillarum, Murex   36 : *6*
anus, Distorsio   84 : *25*
aperta, Trivia   26 : *15*
apicalis, Ancilla   38 : *5*
apiculata, Chiton   112 : *7*
Aplustrum amplustre   16 : *2*
Apollon perca   16 : *29*
  ,,   gyrinus   16 : *12*
Aporrhais occidentalis mainensis   108 : *16*
  ,,   pespelicani   108 : *13*
  ,,   senegalensis   120 : *9*
aprinum, Dentalium   84 : *11*
arabica, Voluta   48 : *3*
arabicula, Cypraea   26 : *11*
aratrum, Strombus   86 : *15*
arausaica, Voluta   43 : *6*
Arca lienosa floridana   126 : *7*
,,   multicostata   126 : *10*
,,   ovalis   126 : *9*
,,   tortuosa   90 : *10*
Architectonica acutissima   82 : *2*
  ,,   granulata 108 : *15* & 16: *25*
  ,,   maxima   82 : *3*
  ,,   nobilis   16 : *25* & 108 : *15*
  ,,   perspectiva   16 : *24*
  ,,   placentalis   118 : *19*
  ,,   trochlearis   82 : *1*
archon, Conus   20 : *9*
arcuatus, Conus   118 : *6*
arcularis, Nassarius   84 : *23*
arenarius, Murex   96 : *4*
arenatus Hwass, Conus   110 : *16*
  ,,   Röd., Conus   130 : *8*
arenosa, Cypraea   30 : *17*
areola, Cassis   88 : *9*
argentata, Patella   14 : *16*
argenteonitens, Lischkeia   16 : *19*
Argobuccinum argus   100 : *15*
  ,,   murrayi   76 : *7*
  ,,   oregonensis   76 : *8*
Argonauta hians   108 : *11*
  ,,   nodosa   115 : *1*
argus, Argobuccinum   100 : *15*

argus, Cypraea   22 : *12*
aristophanes, Conus   110 : *6*
armigera, Thais   102 : *7*
  ,,   , Tudicula   70 : *9*
articularis, Harpa   38 : *18*
articulatus, Phos   118 : *8*
arvanus, Syrinx   112 : *11* & 128 : *11*
asellus, Cypraea   26 : *6*
asianus, Murex   98 :   *3*
asperrimus, Pecten   72 : *15*
astera, Patella   14 : *8*
americana, Astraea   80 : *5*
Astraea americana   80 : *5*
  ,,   aureola   18 : *2*
  ,,   brevispina   18 : *7* & 18 : *10*
  ,,   buschii   18 : *17*
  ,,   calcar   18 : *15* & 18 : *16*
  ,,   heliotropium   18 : *12*
  ,,   imbricata   18 : *14*
  ,,   longispina   18 : *6* & 18 : *19*
  ,,   phoebia   18 : *6* & 19 : *19*
  ,,   pileola   80 : *25*
  ,,   rotularia   80 : *1*
  ,,   stellare   18 : *3*
  ,,   sulcatus   18 : *1*
  ,,   triumphans   18 : *18*
  ,,   tuber   18 : *8*
  ,,   undosa   18 : *13* & 90 : *15*
atlanticus, Conus   60 : *21*
augur, Conus   52 : *10*
Aulica; *see* Voluta
aulica, Voluta   43 : *11* & *12*
Aulicina; *see* Voluta
aulicus, Conus   56 : *5*
aurantia, Cypraea   22 : *3*
  ,,   , Natica   16 : *15*
  ,,   , Pterocera   20 : *13*
aurantiaca, Megapitaria   124 : *5*
aureola, Astraea   18 : *2*
aurisdianae, Strombus   86 : *8*
auris-felis, Cassidula   106 : *21*
auritum, Epitonium   78 : *27*
aurora, Conus   110 : *7*
austini, Conus   120 : *5*
australasium, Charonia   90 : *12*
australis, Ancilla   40 : *14*
  ,,   , Colus   80 : *11*
  ,,   , Conus   54 : *10*
  ,,   , Oliva   40 : *17*

–144–

–162–

—163—